Christian Heroes: Then & Now

CLARENCE JONES

Mr. Radio

CHRISTIAN HEROES: THEN & NOW

CLARENCE JONES

Mr. Radio

JANET & GEOFF BENGE

YWAM PUBLISHING
P.O. BOX 55787 SEATTLE, WA 98155

YWAM Publishing is the publishing ministry of Youth With A Mission (YWAM), an international missionary organization of Christians from many denominations dedicated to presenting Jesus Christ to this generation. To this end, YWAM has focused its efforts in three main areas: (1) training and equipping believers for their part in fulfilling the Great Commission (Matthew 28:19), (2) personal evangelism, and (3) mercy ministry (medical and relief work).

For a free catalog of books and materials, call (425) 771-1153 or (800) 922-2143.
Visit us online at www.ywampublishing.com.

Clarence Jones: Mr. Radio

Published by YWAM Publishing
a ministry of Youth With A Mission
P.O. Box 55787, Seattle, WA 98155-0787

Library of Congress Cataloging-in-Publication Data
Benge, Janet, 1958–
Clarence Jones : Mr. Radio / Janet and Geoff Benge.
p. cm. — (Christian heroes, then & now)
Includes bibliographical references (p.).
ISBN 1-57658-343-0
1. Jones, Clarence W.—Juvenile literature. 2. Missionaries—Ecuador—Biography—Juvenile literature. 3. Missionaries—United States—Biography—Juvenile literature. 4. HCJB (Radio station : Quito, Ecuador)—Biography—
Juvenile literature. 5. Radio in missionary work—Juvenile literature.
I. Benge, Geoff, 1954– II. Title. III. Series.
BV2853.E3J66 2005
266′.0092—dc22 2005016637

Scripture quotations in this book are taken from the King James Version of the Bible.

ISBN 978-1-57658-343-2 (paperback)
ISBN 978-1-57658-621-1 (e-book)

Third printing 2021

Printed in the United States of America

Christian Heroes: Then & Now

Adoniram Judson
Albert Schweitzer
Amy Carmichael
Betty Greene
Brother Andrew
Cameron Townsend
Charles Mulli
Clarence Jones
Corrie ten Boom
Count Zinzendorf
C. S. Lewis
C. T. Studd
David Bussau
David Livingstone
Dietrich Bonhoeffer
D. L. Moody
Elisabeth Elliot
Eric Liddell
Florence Young
Francis Asbury
George Müller
Gladys Aylward
Helen Roseveare
Hudson Taylor
Ida Scudder
Isobel Kuhn
Jacob DeShazer
Jim Elliot
John Flynn
John Newton
John Wesley
John Williams
Jonathan Goforth
Klaus-Dieter John
Lillian Trasher
Loren Cunningham
Lottie Moon
Mary Slessor
Mildred Cable
Nate Saint
Norman Grubb
Paul Brand
Rachel Saint
Richard Wurmbrand
Rowland Bingham
Samuel Zwemer
Sundar Singh
Wilfred Grenfell
William Booth
William Carey

Available in paperback, e-book, and audiobook formats.Unit study curriculum guides are available for select biographies.

www.YWAMpublishing.com

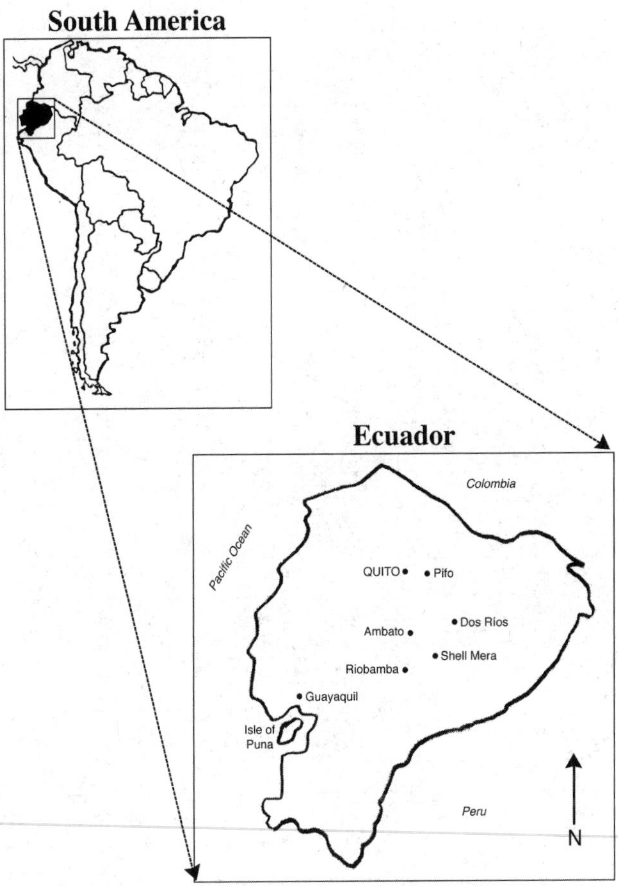
South America
Ecuador
Colombia
Pacific Ocean
QUITO
Pifo
Dos Ríos
Ambato
Shell Mera
Riobamba
Guayaquil
Isle of Puna
Peru
N

Contents

Chapter 1

Doubts

Clarence Jones stared at the latest letter from the United States. The letter painted a dire financial picture. The economic depression was continuing to deepen, and many people who had promised Clarence and his family financial support were now struggling to put food on the table for their own families. In fact, during all of 1932 the Joneses had received only about five hundred dollars in support. It was not nearly enough to provide for the family and keep their ministry going.

Clarence and his wife, Katherine, had done their best to make the money go as far as possible. Clarence had taken two part-time jobs. The family had gone without some of the necessities they were used to and had planted a huge garden in their yard.

From the garden Katherine canned numerous jars of produce. Sometimes that was all the family had to eat. But their best efforts were just not enough, and by mid-1933 Clarence received word that no more support would be coming from the United States for his family or the ministry.

This outcome stunned Clarence. He and his family had given up everything to serve on the mission field. Was it all for nothing? What more could he give? What had gone wrong? Had God really led him to the mission field, or had coming to it been a horrible mistake?

The turmoil Clarence felt about his family's predicament was made all the worse when an electric bill for $6.15 arrived in the mail. Clarence had no money to pay the bill, and without electricity there could be no ministry.

Clarence could feel the knot of worry tightening in his stomach as he laid the bill on the table and stared at it. Would his whole ministry go under because he owed less than seven dollars? To Clarence this seemed likely to happen.

Not knowing what else to do, Clarence walked out to the toolshed at the back of the property. He sat down inside and poured out his heart in prayer. But even as he prayed, the doubts kept coming. Slowly, though, his mind drifted back to his earliest memories as a child. He recalled times when there was little to eat in the house and no money to buy anything. Somehow that had never seemed to dent his parents' faith and trust in God. Now it was as if

Clarence had come full circle. There was little food in the house for his family to eat and no money to buy more, let alone pay the electric bill. Clarence began to think about how his parents might have handled the situation. Those boyhood days in Chicago seemed such a long way away and a long time ago.

Chapter 2

A Member of the Band

Seven-year-old Clarence Jones peered down at the crib. Inside lay a tiny baby with a wrinkly face.

"What do you think of your little brother?" Emma Jones asked.

"Howard's pretty small," Clarence told his mother. He had waited a long time for a brother, but now he was not so sure that this tiny baby in the crib was the kind of brother he needed. Clarence was vaguely aware that there had been two other brothers before him, but they had both died as babies before he was born. It was something his mother did not like to talk about much, but Clarence had overheard her discussing the family tragedies with one of her friends.

From what Clarence had been able to piece together, both his parents had been Salvation Army officers in Duluth, Minnesota, at the time. Winters there were long and brutal, and the only way his parents could make money to buy food was to sell the Salvation Army's magazine, *The War Cry*, for donations. Day after day, Clarence's mother would bundle up first one baby and then the other and leave them to sleep in a washtub by the stove to keep warm while she went to sell *The War Cry* in local bars.

With no money for medicines and little for food, both babies had died from illness. As a result, Clarence was very grateful that his father had taken a job with a steady paycheck in Chicago before Clarence was born on December 15, 1900. However, he was not nearly as grateful for the type of job his father had taken. George Jones was a janitor in a three-story, redbrick apartment building on Chicago's South Side. An apartment came with the job, but it was in the basement of the building and had tiny, rectangular windows too far up the wall for Clarence to see out. To make matters worse, the windows leaked when it rained, and during the harsh winters the snow piled up against them, blocking out the light for weeks at a time.

Clarence was old enough to realize that his father was not paid much money for his labor. His mother bought all of the family's clothes from secondhand stores and meticulously patched and altered them until they were fit to wear. But there never seemed to be enough money to buy long pants for Clarence. Instead Clarence's mother wrapped his legs in old newspapers and tied the papers in place with twine before sending her son off to school on winter mornings. Clarence, though, decided that he would rather freeze to death than look like a walking poster board for the *Chicago Tribune.* As a result, he always ripped the newspaper and twine off his legs as soon as he rounded the corner of the apartment building and was out of his mother's sight.

Now, as he looked down at baby Howard, Clarence felt the very adult concern of how his parents were going to pay for a second child. But somehow, as the weeks and months rolled by, there always seemed to be just enough money for food and even an occasional ice cream.

Almost all of the Jones family activities revolved around the Salvation Army Corps, No. 1, on West Madison Street. Clarence knew that his parents had met when they were young Salvation Army cadets back in Duluth. Joining the Salvation Army had cost his father a lot, since his family had all but disowned him. Clarence had been introduced to Grandmother Jones twice in his life. She was aloof and proper and not a bit like his other grandmother, Bertha Detbrener. Grandma Bertha and Grandpa John gave Clarence something to look forward to every spring: as soon as school was out, Clarence's mother took him and now his young brother Howard to visit them.

Grandma and Grandpa Detbrener lived beside Lake Winnebago in Wisconsin. Getting to their house was a happy adventure from start to finish. From Chicago the family journeyed north by boat up Lake

Michigan to Milwaukee, where they caught a train to Lake Winnebago. As the train rumbled along, Clarence would peer out the window, hoping to catch a glimpse of his grandfather, who was a flagman at a level crossing for the Sault Ste. Marie Railroad Line. His mother had told him that his grandfather had helped to build the railroad but in the process had lost a leg in a construction accident. As a result, the company had made him a flagman.

Summers in Wisconsin were a kaleidoscope of activities for Clarence. Grandpa John understood Clarence's desire to make things, and together they made molds for a whole army of lead soldiers—cavalry and infantrymen, along with their tents and cannons. With the tiny lead figures, Grandpa John would act out war scenes while Clarence watched with rapt interest. Clarence knew that his grandfather, who had emigrated from Germany to Wisconsin, had been a soldier in the Prussian army.

When he was not making something, Clarence passed his time paddling on log rafts or fishing for bullhead in Lake Winnebago. Every lunchtime he had to remember to pick up a five-cent pail of beer from the local tavern and deliver it to his grandfather at work. The beer was thick German beer, and as Clarence carried it, he wondered how anyone could enjoy the taste of such a foul-smelling brew.

While summer was certainly the highlight of his year, Clarence did not mind some things about school. He was a natural athlete and played hockey and baseball with gusto. However, subjects like math and English bored him, and by the time he was fourteen, he'd had enough of school and constant study.

When he was twelve years old, Clarence found his passion—music and, in particular, the E-flat alto horn. Almost everyone in the Salvation Army played a musical instrument of some sort. Clarence's mother played the guitar and tambourine, and his father played the cornet. It did not take Clarence, who had a natural ear for music, long to master the alto horn. Within a year Clarence could play every instrument except the tuba and could substitute for just about every member of the band.

Clarence had just one problem with being in a Salvation Army band. The Army was a religious group, and Clarence had little time for religion. It all seemed a little strange to him. He tried not to get too involved, but being a member of a Salvation Army band made this very difficult. Sometimes at open-air meetings the band would form a circle, and the director, normally Clarence's father, would call for quick testimonies from band members. If no one responded, he would say, "Now then, we'll start here and go right around the circle." Clarence hated being cornered in this way, and when it came his turn to speak, he would always say something vague like, "Ditto to what the last person said," or "That goes for me as well."

Deep in his heart Clarence knew that he would have to resolve the issue of faith sometime, but for now he loved playing music, and he grew to hate school more with each passing day.

As his dislike of studying grew, Clarence began a campaign to get his parents to allow him to leave school. It took a year to finally convince them, and after completing two years of high school, he dropped out. He was fifteen years old and took a job at Montgomery Ward, wrapping and shipping tires. Demand for tires was high because the Great War in Europe was raging. Britain and France were fighting a determined German army, and for the first time in a war, both sides were using motorized vehicles.

This was the first time in his life that Clarence had money of his own to spend. His parents were doing better financially too. His father now worked for Western Electric, and the family had rented a second-floor duplex into which fresh air and sunlight streamed. Clarence thought the family's new home was the height of luxury.

Clarence had his music and his job, and his parents had Howard's education to concentrate on. Everything seemed to be going along well until Clarence became ill with tuberculosis. It was 1918, he was eighteen years old, and the war in Europe was still dragging on when he found himself laid up in bed for six months—six long, boring months during which he had plenty of time to think about where his life was headed.

One day as Clarence was recuperating, Richard Oliver Sr. visited him. Richard had played in the Salvation Army band with Clarence and his father but was now the music director at Moody Church.

The two of them talked for a while about Clarence's illness and how Clarence was feeling. Then Richard looked Clarence in the eye and asked, "I know you play the alto horn, but why don't you come and play the trombone in the band at Moody Church?"

Clarence thought about it for a while and then replied, "I'll do that, as soon as I'm better."

After several weeks, Clarence was feeling well enough to get out of bed and resume his life. Early one Sunday morning he set out for Moody Church and took his place in the band.

Moody Church, located near Chicago's Lincoln Park, was an impressive sight from the outside, but what impressed Clarence more was the size of the church inside. The auditorium seated many hundreds of people, and as Clarence looked out from his place among the band members on stage, the sea of faces packed into the building seemed to go on and on until they disappeared into the gloom at the far reaches of the sanctuary.

As he joined in, Clarence was also impressed by the band. Not only did they play well together, but also, unlike the Salvation Army band, they did not play just hymns. The band at Moody Church also played "Stars and Stripes Forever" and other rousing marches composed by John Philip Sousa.

It was not just the music that impressed Clarence. When Paul Rader, pastor of the church, stood to preach, Clarence was spellbound. Not only was Paul a dynamic speaker, but his words seemed to speak directly to Clarence's heart. Week after week Clarence attended Moody Church to play in the band and listen to the preaching of Paul Rader.

Sunday night, October 27, 1918, was like any other evening service at Moody Church. Clarence was playing the trombone in the band with gusto while the congregation sang along. Finally Paul stood and strode to the pulpit to preach. Clarence laid his trombone aside and sat down to listen to the homily. As usual Paul was in fine form, and the words of his sermon were carefully chosen and hard-hitting—a little too hard-hitting for Clarence. As he listened, Clarence suddenly became aware that in his heart he was a sinner. It did not matter that he had been raised in the Salvation Army and played in the band at Moody Church. In truth, before God he was no better than any of the lowly people he had encountered while playing in the Salvation Army band at the open-air meetings on West Madison Street. Clarence knew that very night that he had to do something about the sinful state of his heart.

When Paul had finished speaking, he invited anyone who wanted to become a Christian to come to the front of the church. From his position on stage with the band, Clarence looked out across the faces of the crowd. People began to make their way to the front of the sanctuary. As they moved, Clarence wondered what people would think when a member of the band stood and walked to the front as well. After all, most people assumed that he was already a Christian. But in the end Clarence decided that it did not matter what people thought. What was more important was responding to what he was feeling in his heart. He rose to his feet, walked to the side of the stage and down the stairs, and joined the others standing at the front of the church with their heads bowed. Finally Paul said a prayer for those who had come forward, and then someone led them to a large room off to the side.

From his association with the Salvation Army, Clarence had seen many dozens of sinners kneel and accept Jesus Christ into their lives. Once he reached the room, Clarence automatically sank to his knees and prayed the sinner's prayer and invited Jesus into his life. Thirty seconds later Clarence was back on his feet and headed out the door to resume his place in the band.

"And where are you going?" a burley man asked as he stepped in front of Clarence.

"I'm leaving. I'm saved now," Clarence replied.

"And how do you know you're saved?" the man asked.

"Because I feel better already," Clarence said.

"What do you mean you feel better now? Suppose you wake up with a toothache tomorrow—what about your salvation then?" the man asked.

Clarence did not quite know what to say, and before he could think of anything, the man continued. "If you're going to last as a Christian, young man, you'll need more than feeling. You'll need to put your feet on the solid rock of God's Word. Let's sit down here for a few minutes and talk."

The man guided Clarence to where two chairs were arranged facing each other. Once they were comfortable, the man opened his worn, leather-bound Bible and began to show Clarence verse after verse about what it meant to be a Christian and how he should live his life to honor God. When they were done, Clarence stood up and headed for the door. "And now, how do you know you're saved?" the man asked again as Clarence was leaving.

"I know I'm saved now because God's Word says so," Clarence replied with a smile on his face.

As he left Moody Church that night, for the first time in his life, Clarence Jones felt sure that his life was on the right track. He had accepted Jesus Christ as his Savior, and he was ready to go anywhere and do anything that God told him to do. The big question he now contemplated was, what exactly would that be?

Chapter 3

A Newfangled Fad

Clarence soon moved his membership from the Salvation Army to Moody Church. His parents and younger brother Howard noticed such a change in Clarence that they, too, soon joined him at Moody Church.

Two weeks after joining the church, Clarence attended a luncheon meeting there. After the meal, a missionary from Japan stood and spoke to the gathered crowd. Clarence was enraptured by the speaker's challenge to missionary service. As soon as an opportunity to respond was presented, Clarence shot up his hand to signify his willingness to become a missionary. His heart thumped in his chest as he surveyed the other hundred or so young people seated around him. Not one of them raised his hand. Clarence could hardly believe it. *God has done so much for each of us,* he thought. *Surely we should want to do what little we can for Him.* The missionary waited for others to respond, but Clarence's hand remained the only one raised. Finally Clarence could no longer hold in the excitement he was feeling, and he blurted out for all to hear, "I've got Christ as my Savior. I'll be glad to do anything He wants, go anyplace He sends me."

The missionary beamed at Clarence's response and then said a prayer before dismissing the group.

As Clarence bicycled home that day, he thought about what he had said. He did want to serve God, and he did not care how difficult it was—he was sure of that. But he did not have many qualifications. He was a good musician and liked working with children, but he had dropped out of high school to work packing tires for Montgomery Ward. Clarence peddled on, thinking about his options, when all of a sudden a thought lit up his mind: Go to Moody Bible Institute!

By the time Clarence reached the family apartment, he was sure that this was the next step God had for him. What he was not sure about was whether he could complete that step. Now that he was nearly eighteen years old, could he really go back to school and study hard enough to pass the courses? Clarence was not at all sure he could, but he knew he had to try his best. So after work the following day, he took the bus to Moody Bible Institute, where he talked with a secretary.

"What course do you want to take?" the secretary asked him.

"Why, the missionary one, of course!" Clarence replied.

The secretary laughed. "You are eager, aren't you! We don't have a course specifically for missionaries, but we do have some good classes that would be very helpful for a missionary."

That was close enough for Clarence. That night he enrolled at the Bible institute in a three-year study program that would start in six weeks, at the beginning of 1919. The next day he handed in his notice at work.

Mr. and Mrs. Jones were delighted when Clarence told them about his next step. In fact, his mother burst into tears. "I've been praying for a long time for you to do some more training for the Lord," she told her older son.

Clarence was even more delighted when he learned that three of his friends had also enrolled at Moody Bible Institute. They were Richard Oliver Jr., Lance Latham, and Howard Ferrin, who had all played with him in the band at Moody Church.

As the first day of class rolled around, Clarence was filled with both excitement and dread—excitement at what lay ahead and dread as to whether or not he could pass his classes. He soon discovered that he did not have to be concerned about passing the courses. Now that he was studying things that interested him, Clarence was soon earning straight A's. Not only that—he was also a natural leader, and by the time his third year at Moody Bible Institute rolled around, he was elected class president.

Before he knew it, Clarence's three years at Moody were over, and he graduated in 1921, just after celebrating his twenty-first birthday. Now that he had some formal training, Clarence was ready to take on a new challenge. This came in the form of a tent crusade with a well-known evangelist named Charles Neighbour. Together they headed down through the coal-mining district of West Virginia, pitching a large tent and preaching to the curious crowds that would gather in it each night. Clarence found tremendous satisfaction in playing the trombone and leading the singing at the tent meetings while Charles preached.

When their time in West Virginia was up, the two men headed for home, preaching as they went. Along the way they stopped for the night at the home of the Reverend Adam Welty. Mr. Welty ran a rescue mission for down-and-outs in the small town of Lima, Ohio. Clarence was impressed with the man's dedication to his mission, but he was even more impressed with his beautiful sixteen-year-old daughter, Katherine.

Clarence's heart pounded the first time he saw Katherine coming down the stairs, and he could not wait to get to know her better. This proved difficult because Katherine's mother had died when Katherine was three years old, and Katherine's father was extremely protective of his daughter. Clarence soon discovered that there was no way he would be allowed to speak to Katherine unchaperoned, and so he resigned himself to talking to her in group situations.

Even so, Clarence managed to find out quite a lot about Katherine and the Welty family. Katherine's uncle was a United States senator, and Katherine had a sister, Ruth, and two older brothers, Fred, a senior tenor in the Westminster choir, and Roy, a Princeton graduate and lawyer.

The day he and Charles left Lima, Clarence knew he wanted to come back and spend more time with Katherine. But when he told his friends back in Chicago that he was smitten with a sixteen-year-old girl, they teased him mercilessly. "With all the girls here in Chicago, why did you have to fall for a high school student in Lima?"

Clarence could not answer the question. He just knew that there was something special about Katherine. He began to send her letters and elaborately illustrated love poems. She in turn wrote to him about her life. She told Clarence that she had won a typing contest for the western half of Ohio and that she had been offered a scholarship in literature and creative writing at Harvard University, although she had her heart set on becoming a concert pianist. Clarence was concerned that Katherine might go to Harvard and lose interest in their friendship, and he wished he could visit her more often. But he was too busy traveling with Charles to make a trip to Lima.

All of that changed, however, in April 1922, when Clarence received a telegram from his old music master at Moody Church, Richard Oliver Sr. The telegram read, "Paul Rader starting new tabernacle. Will you come and play in brass quartet?"

The thought of working with a man of Paul Rader's spiritual stature thrilled Clarence, who sent back a return telegram agreeing to take the position. Once he was back in Chicago, Clarence learned the details of why Paul had left Moody Church. The split revolved around Paul's overarching interest in evangelism. Over the years Paul had clashed with the elders of Moody Church, who felt he was devoting too much of his time and energy to evangelism and not enough to running the church. In the time that Clarence had been out on the road with Charles Neighbour, things had come to a head, and Paul had stepped down from his position of pastor at Moody Church. Paul's intention had been to start an evangelistic program in New York City, but those plans had fallen through. Instead Paul began running tent meetings on the North Side of Chicago. These meetings had proved to be so popular that Paul decided to stay in Chicago and turn the tent at the corner of Barry, Clark, and Halsted Streets into a permanent structure, which soon became known as the Chicago Gospel Tabernacle.

The Chicago Gospel Tabernacle looked more like a barn than a church. It was an enormous wooden structure that seated five thousand people on hard, straight-back wooden benches. The walls inside were not painted, and the structure had no floor, just sawdust spread on the ground. Several large potbelly stoves were used to heat the place. From the first time he set foot in the tabernacle, Clarence knew he belonged there.

Each night more and more people poured into the building for the evening service, and the atmosphere was electric with anticipation. Not only was Paul Rader a great preacher, but he was also adept at using music to prepare the audience for the message he was going to deliver. Each service started with rousing singing and musical numbers. Clarence's two friends, Richard Oliver Jr. and Lance Latham, often played duets on twin grand pianos arranged onstage. It was not long before Clarence and the quartet were enthralling the crowd with their playing. Clarence's brother, Howard, a gifted cornet player and still only a teenager, was also a member of the quartet. He and Clarence often played duets, blending their instruments as they offered up stirring renditions of popular gospel tunes. Their most popular duet was "Christ Alone," which they first played together at an Easter sunrise service and which was soon being requested almost every night.

Clarence often smiled to himself as he played the trombone at the tabernacle. While Paul, along with his gospel campaign, was taking Chicago by storm, the approach he was using was not that much different from what Clarence had experienced growing up in the Salvation Army. And as he had done at Moody Church, Clarence loved to lay his instrument aside after the music was over and listen to Paul's inspired and dynamic preaching. He was amazed by the way Paul seemed to throw himself physically and emotionally into every sermon he preached. Paul was usually so drenched from perspiration at the end of each service that he had to take a shower.

While the ministry of the Chicago Gospel Tabernacle was proving to be very effective, Paul Rader was not a man to rest on his laurels. On June 12, 1922, he asked Clarence and the other members of the quartet to stay behind after the evening service. As they waited for the tabernacle to empty and for Paul to appear, the quartet members discussed the next week's program, though Clarence was certain that they were all wondering why Paul had asked them to stay late.

Finally Paul arrived, still sweating from delivering his sermon, and the five men got chairs and huddled together near the front of the building. The janitor came by to rake the sawdust, but Paul asked him to start at the back so that they could have some privacy.

Once they were all seated, Paul came straight to the point. "God has brought a wonderful opportunity to us, boys!" he began. "Finally we are going to get to fight Satan in his own territory—the air!"

Clarence's mind raced, but he could not imagine what Paul meant. He glanced at his three friends, who looked just as baffled.

Paul chuckled. "Mayor Thompson called on me this afternoon and asked if we could provide some musicians for the new radio station that is starting in Chicago. What do you think?"

Clarence did not know what to think. He had read about radio, but he had not actually heard one himself. Radios were mainly in the hands of ham radio operators and were used to pass messages along, but he had read that some men were trying to broadcast radio programs so that anyone could pick them up if they had a receiver.

Paul talked on over Clarence's thoughts. "The Bible tells us that Satan has dominion over the air, but we are about to launch an assault on his work. We'll take our gospel songs right into the homes, the hotels, the saloons—everywhere there is a receiver—and we'll proclaim the good news to men and women who would never think of setting foot in a church."

Paul's enthusiasm was contagious, and within a few minutes he had convinced the four young men that this was a wonderful new opportunity for spreading the gospel. However, once news got around that Paul Rader and the Tabernacle Quartet were about to go on the radio, many Christians became upset.

"How could God possibly bless this newfangled fad?" they asked. "Radio is a toy that's not going to last, so why waste the Lord's money on such a foolish venture?" And, "Who does it reach anyway? Does the average family have a receiver in their living room, and are they ever likely to buy one? Of course not!"

Still, Paul was confident that radio had a future. And so with the quartet's approval, he signed them up to deliver their first radio broadcast. The broadcast was scheduled for a week later on Saturday, June 17, 1922.

A blustery wind blew in across Lake Michigan as Paul Rader and the Tabernacle Quartet climbed to the roof of City Hall in downtown Chicago, where the studio of the fledgling radio station WHT was located. Clarence had expected something grand, and he was surprised to discover that the studio was in fact a small booth constructed of bare pine boards. It didn't even have a roof. An engineer ushered them into the booth and pointed them to a small hole cut into one of the walls. "Point your instruments toward that hole, and when we say play, you play," he instructed.

The members of the quartet took out their instruments, faced the wall with the hole, and waited for the instruction to play. Several minutes later someone pushed what appeared to be the mouthpiece from a telephone through the hole, and the engineer said, "Play."

Clarence pressed the trombone to his lips and blew for all he was worth. With the wind whistling around them and the noise of traffic filtering up from the street below, Clarence wondered how anyone listening to the radio would be able to hear what they were playing, but he played heartily anyway. After they had played several rousing gospel tunes, Paul stepped forward, and facing the hole in the wall as the quartet had, he began to preach. When he was done preaching, the quartet played one more tune, and the broadcast was over.

As he climbed down from the roof of City Hall, Clarence wondered whether their playing and Paul's preaching had actually been heard by anyone in Chicago. He did not have to wait long to find out. Back at the tabernacle office, the telephone was ringing off the hook with listeners wanting to know when Paul was going to preach on the air again and making musical requests for the quartet to play on the next broadcast.

The response of the radio audience startled Clarence, but Paul reacted with the confidence of someone who had expected it all along. As the weeks went by, the new radio ministry grew at a startling rate. Soon the Chicago Gospel Tabernacle was broadcasting on the radio each Sunday for fourteen hours straight as well as daily from 7:00 AM to 8:00 AM on the newly formed Columbia Broadcasting System (CBS).

Clarence loved everything about this new way of reaching out with the gospel, and soon he found himself promoted to the position of program director. His days were hectic as he lined up piano duets, brass quartets, soloists, and preachers to fill in the many hours of radio broadcasting each week. Since there was no way to record any of the programming in advance and play it back at a later time, all of the musicians and speakers had to be in front of the microphone at broadcast time.

Despite his duties as program director and member of the Tabernacle Quartet, Clarence managed to find the time to continue pursuing Katherine Welty, who was now studying at Nyack Bible Training College in New York state. Whenever it was possible, he would catch a train to New York and surprise Katherine after class. Gradually, as the two of them continued to see each other, Katherine's father began to warm to the idea of Clarence's marrying his daughter.

Sensing this change, Clarence decided one night to propose to Katherine. Much to his relief, nineteen-year-old Katherine agreed to be his bride. Clarence could hardly wait for their wedding day to roll around.

Chapter 4

"Go South—with Radio"

After a short engagement, just long enough to plan a simple wedding, Clarence Jones and Katherine Welty were married at the Welty home in Lima, Ohio, on August 2, 1924. Clarence's family, along with Clarence's two closest friends, Lance Latham and Richard Oliver Jr., made the trek to Lima to attend the marriage ceremony. Lance played the piano, and Richard served as best man, while Paul Rader conducted the ceremony.

During the ceremony Clarence tried not to worry, but inside he was a little nervous, not because he was marrying Katherine but because he had no spare cash and no plans for his honeymoon. When he had prayed about the situation, he had felt a peace that God would take care of everything. He just wished he had known a little more about how God was going to take care of it before the wedding service started.

In fact, Clarence was so absorbed in thinking about the dilemma that he failed to notice that the young ringbearer had dropped the ring and Richard was now down on his knees searching for it. To cover the action going on at the altar, Paul had launched into a long prayer, praying not only for Clarence and Katherine but also for just about everyone else he knew around the world. At the same time that Clarence was coming to the conclusion that Paul's prayer was better suited to a missionary prayer meeting than a wedding service, he felt a tap on his ankle. Startled, he looked down to see Richard motioning for him to lift his foot. Clarence obliged, and there was the missing ring right under his shoe. With the ring in hand, Paul quickly brought his prayer to a close and continued with the rest of the service.

During the wedding reception that followed, Clarence was still fretting about the uncertainty of the honeymoon destination, when Paul motioned to him. Clarence walked across the room to Paul, who quickly pressed a wad of cash into his hand. "This is for you to go to Baltimore. Take a couple of days for a honeymoon, then set up tent meetings for us there," he told Clarence.

Clarence was relieved and was finally able to enjoy the rest of the wedding reception. When it was over, the newlyweds set off for Baltimore in a borrowed car.

Clarence and Katherine enjoyed a wonderful weekend together. Then Clarence got down to the business of finding a suitable central site on which to erect the 150 x 60 foot tent and began rallying people to attend the upcoming campaign. Once a site was secured and the tent put up, Paul arrived from Chicago to conduct what turned out to be some of the largest Christian services ever held in Baltimore. During the campaign many people were challenged to accept the gospel message.

From Baltimore, Clarence and Katherine drove on to Atlantic City, where once again Clarence set up a meeting place and a schedule for Paul to come and preach. When those meetings were finally over, Clarence and Katherine made their way to Chicago to set up home together. Clarence was soon hard at work again as program director for the radio broadcasts and playing once more in the Tabernacle Quartet.

Paul was continually pushing Clarence and the radio team to be more creative, often putting them on the spot to see what they could come up with. One night, as he was preaching a sermon on the Walls of Jericho, he would stop, point to Clarence, and expect him and the quartet to come up with the appropriate sound effect. The members of the quartet found themselves blowing fanfares on their instruments and stomping in unison to simulate the sound of marching. On one occasion Clarence even found himself drawing a violin bow across a handsaw to simulate the sound of rushing wind. At first it seemed a little tacky to Clarence, but to his surprise, when it was all put together on radio, somehow the sound effects seemed to engage the listener more.

The musicians were also encouraged to write new songs for the various shows, and Clarence rose to the occasion, contributing thirty of his own songs. Some of the songs became the most requested tunes played on the air. There were times on a radio broadcast when Clarence not only had written the music but also introduced it to the audience, played the trombone as it was being performed, and led the orchestra.

The amount of coordination for the radio broadcasts was enormous, and soon Clarence had to hire twenty-five telephone operators to handle all of the calls the programs generated.

Many of the listeners to the radio broadcasts joined the Chicago Gospel Tabernacle, and the five thousand seats in the sanctuary were soon filled to capacity for each service. Fifty musicians played in the orchestra each Sunday, and a three-hundred-member choir sang for the congregation. As one of the largest churches in the United States, the Chicago Gospel Tabernacle experienced a constant push to pioneer other new areas of ministry besides radio. Paul Rader had a vision to organize boys' and girls' clubs, much like Scouts but with a Christian emphasis. Once again he turned to Clarence to lead the new work.

Clarence gladly accepted this new challenge, though he resigned himself to getting less sleep, since he still had the tabernacle's radio ministry to run. He invited his old friends Richard and Lance, along with Virginia Highfield, to help him with the boys' and girls' clubs, and soon the four of them were hard at work designing the new program. News about what they were doing spread quickly, and soon thousands of boys and girls between the ages of eight and fifteen were meeting each Saturday afternoon at the Chicago Gospel Tabernacle.

When summer arrived, Clarence rented a campground across Lake Michigan at Berrien Springs, Michigan, and the boys went camping.

Paul had such confidence in Clarence's ability to get things done that when the Chicago Gospel Tabernacle bought its own conference ground near Muskegon Heights, Michigan, he asked Clarence to oversee the ministry there as well.

Again Clarence accepted the challenge, but it took much of his youthful energy to keep everything running smoothly. He was also kept busy at home. By now Katherine had borne two bouncing, blonde daughters. Marian was born in 1925 and Marjorie in 1927.

Despite the hectic schedule, Clarence felt satisfied with his life, until one night in early summer 1927. The Jones family was staying at the conference ground near Muskegon Heights, where Paul was delivering a series of messages to those attending a summer camp. Clarence played his trombone in the band on Sunday morning as the campers joined in some rousing singing, and then Paul stood and spoke about the need for missionaries around the world.

Until this point, Clarence and Katherine had considered themselves "home missionaries," especially since thousands of people were hearing the gospel for the first time through the Chicago Gospel Tabernacle and its ever-expanding radio ministry. But this morning as Paul spoke, Clarence felt a strange stirring in his heart. Even though he was the camp director and music leader, at the end of the service, Clarence felt that he should go forward to the altar and surrender his life to missionary service. Clarence couldn't help but notice how stunned Paul looked as he put down his trombone and made his way to join the others at the front.

"Well, God bless you," Paul said to Clarence after praying with him. "We need you here in this work, but if God wants you in missionary work, then that's what we want for you as well."

Clarence was grateful for Paul's encouraging words, and after the service he returned to the cabin where Katherine had stayed to look after their two daughters. He decided not to say anything to her about what he had done until he was sure he was doing what God wanted him to do.

Later that week two missionaries came to speak at the camp. They were a young couple in their late twenties who had been working in Tibet. Both of their children had died in Tibet as a result of the harsh conditions. Despite the grief they felt, the couple had continued serving God there. The missionary couple's story touched Clarence deeply, and he began to pray that God would direct him to a specific country where he, too, could serve as a missionary.

That night, as Clarence sat in the meeting at camp, he heard a voice saying to him, "Arise and go south—with radio." The voice was so clear and startling that Clarence immediately looked around the room to see whether anyone else had heard it, but no one seemed to be reacting to the strange occurrence. Clarence sat stunned. He had prayed for a specific country to go to, but he felt that God had instead given him a direction in which to go—south. He drew a mental map in his head and came up with about twenty countries south of Michigan. How would he know which country he was meant to go to? And with radio! What did that mean, especially since at that time there were few radio receivers in either Central or South America?

Despite the questions, excitement rose in Clarence as he thought about the possibilities of taking radio overseas. But as quickly as his excitement arose, his heart sank when he contemplated telling Katherine, who was struggling with two small children. Clarence was sure that there was no way Katherine would be willing to leave the United States to "go south with radio." Katherine had made it quite clear from the outset of their marriage that being a home missionary was challenging enough for her.

As he drank his nightly cup of cocoa before heading back to the cabin, Clarence felt sick to his stomach. He had prayed for guidance and had gotten it.

But now he was unsure what would happen next. He decided not to tell Katherine about the guidance right away. Instead he spent much of the night in bed concerned about her reaction to this new direction in life.

By the time breakfast rolled around the next morning, Clarence knew that he had to tell his wife what was going through his mind. He pushed his poached egg around the plate a few times with his fork and then began. "Katherine, if the Lord were to call us to the mission field together, would you go?"

Katherine got up from her chair and walked around the table to Clarence. She wrapped her arms about him. "It's all right, dear," she said gently. "Last night, when I was putting the girls to bed and you were at the service, the Lord came to me, and He asked me very plainly, 'Katherine, will you go?'"

Tears streamed down Clarence's cheeks as he listened to what his wife was telling him. Surely everything would go smoothly now that God had led them both into mission work. Little did Clarence dream of the obstacles that lay on the path ahead for him and Katherine.

Chapter 5

Going South

Clarence dreaded one task—telling Paul of his and Katherine's decision to "go south with radio." Clarence had been Paul's right-hand man for five years now, and he knew how much Paul relied on him. Still, he had to tell him, and so when the family returned to Chicago from Muskegon Heights, Clarence gathered his courage. He met Paul in the tabernacle hallway after the Sunday evening service. "I have to tell you something," he said to Paul. "Katherine and I have been called to be missionaries. We have prayed about it together and separately, and we are sure of it."

"Wonderful, wonderful!" Paul said as he gave Clarence a congratulatory slap on the back. "Just what I was hoping to hear. Since I learned that you have a missionary call on your life, I've been eyeing just the right place for you to serve. I believe it's India. There is much to be done to bring the gospel to that dark land. Why, my own daughter Pauline believes that God is calling her to serve there."

"But, Mr. Rader," Clarence replied, "God is not calling me to India. He is calling me south to Latin America."

Clarence watched as the smile lines on Paul's face hardened. "You won't consider helping me in India, then?" Paul asked.

"I'm afraid not," Clarence said. "It was a specific call to take radio and go south."

"Oh," Paul said. "Then I guess you will be going out on your own."

Clarence could not think of an adequate reply to the statement. He could hear something final in Paul's voice that seemed to say "good-bye" and "I'm not going to give you my blessing" all in one. Clarence watched as Paul walked past him and on down the hallway, shaking hands with various people as he went. It was a bittersweet moment, a moment in which Clarence knew that his ten-year relationship with Paul Rader had been forever altered.

While Clarence was a little shocked at the lack of encouragement he received from Paul, he was determined to continue on and pursue his call to missions. That night, after the girls were asleep, he and Katherine got out an atlas and peered at it. A dizzying array of countries lay to the south of the

United States. There were enormous ones like Brazil and Argentina, a long, thin one called Chile, and tiny states huddled together like Panama, Costa Rica, and El Salvador. The question that Clarence and Katherine asked themselves was, which one of these was ready for a Christian radio station?

The answer did not come like a flash in the night, and Clarence and Katherine set about examining their options. Eventually they settled on Venezuela as the most likely candidate for a place to set up a Christian radio station. Things began to fall into place when Clarence learned that the Scandinavian Alliance Mission worked in the country. He sent in an application to serve with the mission and convinced his brother-in-law, Chet Churchill, to go with him to Venezuela on an exploratory trip. Chet, who was married to Katherine's sister Ruth, was in construction and at the time was looking for business opportunities in South America, and he was happy to accompany Clarence.

The two men set sail from New York City on February 1, 1928. Neither man could speak a word of Spanish, but that did not daunt them. On the way to board the ship, they stopped off to buy a Spanish-English dictionary to help them communicate when they got to Venezuela.

Clarence found his first ocean voyage to be more challenging than he had anticipated. He battled seasickness as the swelling waves lifted the ship high and then receded, leaving the vessel to crash back down into the trough between the waves. Despite the queasiness in his stomach, Clarence, with the aid of Chet, held daily Bible studies for the other passengers, and he entertained them at dinner by playing his trombone. Clarence soon learned that most of their fellow passengers were headed south to seek their fortunes in the newly opened oil fields of Venezuela.

Six days after setting out from New York, the ship reached Puerto Rico, where everyone was allowed to go ashore. Once on dry land, Clarence found it almost impossible to stay steady on his feet. He had become so used to the rocking motion of the ship that the ground seemed to move under him, causing him to stagger along the main street. Eventually he fell flat on his face in the gutter. Clarence lay there with his eyes shut for a moment. When he turned his head and looked up, a police officer was standing over him. Clarence knew that he must appear to the officer to be drunk. At the same time, he noticed Chet frantically reaching into his pocket for the Spanish-English dictionary. Using gestures and pointing to words in the dictionary, Chet was eventually able to convince the police officer that his brother-in-law was not a derelict but was a man who had been at sea so long that he had lost his "land legs." Finally the officer waved his hand and walked on. Chet then helped Clarence onto his feet and guided him back to the ship.

Although Clarence seemed to be having trouble with his land legs, he began to get his sea legs on the second part of the voyage to Venezuela. Soon he was enjoying strolling along the deck at midnight, watching the moon and stars reflect off the water of the Caribbean Sea.

Finally, several days after the ship had set out from Puerto Rico, the coast of Venezuela came into view. Clarence stood at the rail of the ship and gazed out at the lush, green foliage that stretched up from sea level to inland mountains. The jungle was denser than any forest Clarence had ever seen. As the ship steamed along parallel to the coastline, a small village came into view. The red- and brown-roofed houses of the village were painted in bright colors and were nestled together at the edge of a narrow beach. The place looked almost idyllic to Clarence, who watched transfixed as small fishing boats plied the bright-blue ocean water off the village. By late afternoon the ship was tied up alongside the dock at La Guira Harbor. Clarence and Chet planned to head into Caracas, Venezuela's capital, the following morning.

As the early morning sun stretched its rays across La Guira Harbor, Clarence and Chet disembarked and were driven to Caracas. The road they were on was concrete and in much better condition than Clarence had imagined it would be as it snaked its way from sea level up into the mountains. As it switched back and forth on itself, it afforded Clarence and Chet wonderful panoramic views across La Guira and the Caribbean beyond. Finally they crossed over the mountain ridge and descended to Caracas, located 3,300 feet above sea level.

From Caracas, Clarence and Chet began a tour of Venezuela, staying with missionaries serving with the Scandinavian Alliance Mission and the Christian and Missionary Alliance. At one of the missionary homes they stayed in, renovations were under way to provide room for four missionaries coming to serve in the country. Clarence decided to stay there for a week, climbing out of bed at the crack of dawn and helping with the renovation project.

Many of the missionaries Clarence and Chet stayed with were working among the various and sometimes remote Indian tribes. Clarence loved to pull his polished trombone from its case and play it in many of the Indian villages they visited. Most of the Indians had never seen such an instrument before, and they laughed and giggled with delight as Clarence played.

As a musician, Clarence was fascinated by the small brass bands that seemed to be the center of entertainment in many of the small towns they passed through. The bands would gather in the town square in the evenings and play for all their worth on instruments that were tarnished and often dented and battered. Clarence had to admit that although the musicians were enthusiastic, the quality of the music they produced was not always very good. What did capture his interest was the way most of the bands had two drummers, who seemed to try to outdo each other in their playing, banging on the drums in often intricate and unusual rhythm patterns.

On one occasion, as Clarence and Chet were being driven over a steep mountain pass by a missionary, the Model T Ford they were riding in ran out of fuel. Clarence and Chet accompanied the missionary as he walked back along the road to a small village they had passed through. There was no gas station in the village, but the missionary managed to convince many of the local residents to drain the kerosene from their lamps into a can. The men carried the can back to the Model T and poured its contents into the car's gas tank. Clarence had to admit that he was a little dubious about this solution to their predicament. After all, back home he had never heard of anyone running a Model T on kerosene. To his surprise, when the missionary cranked the engine, the car burst into life. Clarence and Chet quickly climbed in, and they were off on their way again. When they reached the cloud-shrouded summit of the mountain pass, the missionary turned off the engine, and the Model T coasted for three hours down the other side of the mountain.

Clarence and Chet also visited Venezuela's oil fields located along the edges of Lake Maracaibo. The place was a buzz of activity as new oil wells were frantically being drilled. From the oil fields they headed back to Caracas, where through his contacts, one of the missionaries they had stayed with had been able to arrange a meeting with the president of Venezuela.

Since the government of a country controlled the airways of that country, Clarence knew he would need the backing of the Venezuelan government to start a Christian radio station in Venezuela. Of course, since Clarence felt that God had led him to Venezuela, he expected such permission to be merely a formality. So when he asked President Gomez for permission to build a noncommercial, nondenominational radio station and explained how it would bring news and culture along with the Word of God to the airways of Venezuela, he was surprised when the president shook his head. "You would be on the air, filling it with all kinds of things that would turn my people against me. We have no place for foreigners on the air here. We have our own religion," President Gomez told Clarence.

Stung by this setback, Clarence and Chet decided to travel on to Colombia, hoping that the government there would be more open to a Christian radio station. But as in Venezuela, the government turned Clarence down, telling him once again that there was no place for foreigners on the airways in their country.

His spirit beginning to flag, Clarence moved on to Panama and then to Cuba, hoping that the governments there would grant him the permission he needed. But as in Venezuela and Colombia, the governments of both of these countries refused his request.

After seven weeks away, Clarence returned home to Chicago, dejected and with more questions than answers. Had he wasted his money on a pointless trip? Had he let his enthusiasm get ahead of his better judgment? And more important, had he really heard the voice of God telling him to go, or had it been his own mind? Clarence wished he knew the answers to these questions, but he didn't, and he felt depressed and discouraged.

Katherine, on the other hand, having been alone with the two children for seven weeks and now pregnant with their third child, seemed to Clarence to be relieved that they would not be going anywhere right away. The initial zeal she had felt when God first spoke to her about going as a missionary had faded, and now she urged Clarence to forget the entire episode in their lives and again focus his energy on his ministry at the Chicago Gospel Tabernacle.

Eighteen months later, Clarence was as busy as ever at the Chicago Gospel Tabernacle. Despite all this activity, he could find no peace. Katherine had given birth to a son, but he had been a sickly child and had lived for only two days. The death of his newborn son deeply saddened Clarence, as did the fact that he still had no idea what going south with radio meant. And until he could figure that out, he resisted Paul's urging that he and Katherine go to India and become missionaries there. This action put a distance between him and Paul that Clarence, despite his best efforts, could not bridge. Finally, in frustration and desperation, Clarence decided to give it all up—his vision for radio in South America and his work at the Chicago Gospel Tabernacle. Instead, he would join the United States navy.

Chapter 6

A New Plan of Action

"What do you mean the navy won't take me?" Clarence asked the recruiting officer.

"Well, we can afford to be selective," the officer replied apologetically. "What with the Wall Street crash and everything, a lot of men are trying to sign up. We're only taking men with 20/20 vision, and yours is far from that."

Clarence could not believe it. He had been sure that with his radio experience the navy would scoop him up and put him to work in a radio transmission room somewhere. But they did not want him, even with his radio experience.

As he walked toward the bus stop, Clarence felt an even worse failure than before. How was he going to support his family now? He still had his job at the Chicago Gospel Tabernacle, but ever since coming back from Venezuela, he had found it increasingly difficult to pump up the enthusiasm he needed to keep the work running smoothly. As the bus wound its way through the streets of Chicago, Clarence brooded on what he would tell Katherine when he arrived home.

Clarence wearily climbed the stairs of the apartment building, still not sure how to break the news to Katherine that he had been rejected by the navy. He had to wait for several minutes on the second-floor landing because someone was moving into one of the empty apartments. He gave a nod to a woman carrying a box of books, and then he looked again. "Ruth Miller?" he asked.

The woman turned and smiled at him. "Why, it's Clarence Jones! How wonderful to see you again."

"Are you moving in?" Clarence asked, realizing that it was rather obvious that she was.

"Yes, my husband and I are on furlough for a year, and we're using Chicago as a base. Oh, my name's Ruth Clark now. I married an Englishman born in Jamaica, and we have two children. How about you?"

"You know Katherine, of course, and we have two children, both girls. We'll have to have you up for dinner soon," Clarence replied.

"Wonderful," Ruth said. "I'd love to catch up with you both and tell you about our missionary work in Ecuador."

Clarence nodded and continued on up the stairs. He felt in a better mood now. Ruth had helped with the boys' and girls' clubs Clarence had established at the Chicago Gospel Tabernacle, and he remembered her as always being full of faith for what God could do. Perhaps, he hoped, some of Ruth's faith would rub off on his family.

A week later the Clark family were seated around the table with Clarence, Katherine, and their two girls. Ruth's husband, John, who was director of the Christian and Missionary Alliance Bible school in Ambato, Ecuador, regaled them with tales from Ecuador.

"You should see the countryside," John told them. "It has everything from snowcapped volcanoes to tangled, green jungles, where trees grow a foot a day, to luxurious white, sandy beaches."

"It sounds quite a bit like Venezuela," Clarence blurted out. Instantly he regretted the comment. He did not like to talk about his failed trip south in search of a base for a radio ministry.

"Have you been to Venezuela?" Ruth asked.

"A while back, visiting missionaries," Clarence replied flatly, and then changed the subject. "So tell us what's the most exciting thing you've seen happening in Ecuador."

John Clark's eyes lit up. "That would have to be the Larsons' work. It's quite amazing."

"Yes," Ruth chimed in. "They are from Wisconsin, and they've been missionaries for only five years, but it's amazing what they've accomplished in that time. They live southeast of Quito on the edge of the jungle. Things were a little slow at first, but they kept plodding on, and now they have incredible favor with the locals and the government."

"Such as?" Clarence asked.

"I won't be able to list everything," John began, "but I know the government has asked Reuben Larson to oversee development in the whole eastern part of the country, from the Andes east; they call the area the Oriente. Reuben is in charge of road building and banking there as well."

"And don't forget about the salt sales," Ruth interjected.

"Oh, yes—they are very important. There's no natural source of salt in the jungle, and the government regulates its sale. It's a very key position, since everyone wants salt," John said.

"That's a lot to accomplish in five years," Katherine commented as she excused the children from the table so they could go play in the living room.

"It sure is. And they have big plans for the future. In fact, they are coming home on furlough in a couple of months. Why don't you book them to speak at the tabernacle, Clarence? That way you could hear them yourself," Ruth suggested.

"That's a good idea," Clarence said. "I think I'll do just that. We're always looking for inspiring missionary speakers, especially for the young people."

The two couples continued to chat, and Ruth promised to find out who was handling Reuben and

Grace Larson's itinerary while they were home on furlough. Clarence could then contact that person and make arrangements for the Larsons to speak at the Chicago Gospel Tabernacle.

Clarence did just that, and the Larsons' contact wrote back to confirm that the couple would be able to speak at the church. As it turned out, however, Clarence and Katherine met Grace Larson before she and her husband ever showed up at the Chicago Gospel Tabernacle.

The Joneses were taking a short vacation in Omaha, Nebraska. Clarence called it a working holiday because he was leading the singing at the Omaha Gospel Tabernacle for the weekend. The speaker at the Sunday evening service was Grace Larson. Clarence sat and listened intently as Grace spoke about their missionary work in Ecuador.

"It was very difficult at first," Grace said. "We established a small trading post on the edge of the jungle. We planned to use the trading post as a way to develop relationships with the local Indians so that we could share the gospel with them. But the Indians would run in and buy what they wanted and run out again."

Grace went on to explain that after several months she and Reuben felt completely defeated. They had not yet been able to share the gospel with one Indian. In desperation, one Sunday morning the two of them got down on their knees and prayed, asking God to show them how to break through to the Indians or else to let them leave. As they prayed, they both felt the Lord encourage them with a verse from Zechariah 4:6: "Not by might, nor by power, but by my spirit."

"Years before, this verse had been our motto, but in our busyness we had somehow lost sight of it," Grace said. "We were greatly encouraged to know that we were not alone in our endeavor. The very next morning we experienced that most amazing breakthrough. Two Indians in dugout canoes came down the river and pulled up at the trading post. 'People have been told many bad things about you,' they said, 'but we have been watching you, and they are lies. We want to help you clear the land and build a better house.' From that day on, God began to show us great favor among the Indians."

Before she finished speaking, Grace made a stirring call for all those who felt called to missions to come to the altar at the front of the auditorium. Then she turned to Clarence and said, "Will you please lead the singing for the altar call."

Clarence looked sheepishly back at her. "I'm sorry, I can't," he replied. "I'm going to the altar myself!"

As one of the other musicians led the singing, Clarence left the platform and walked to the altar. Grace Larson's words had deeply touched him. The Larsons had persevered in the face of many challenges and great difficulties, and God had been faithful to them. In trying to establish a Christian radio station in Latin America, Clarence had faced many challenges and difficulties. But instead of trusting God, he had allowed those things to pile up and eventually bring him down and sap his faith. With his eyes closed and his head bowed, Clarence rededicated his life to missionary service.

After the service, Clarence and Katherine took Grace out for a milk shake. "Have you ever thought about using radio in Ecuador?" Clarence asked casually as they sipped their milk shakes.

Grace's eyes lit up. "Yes, it's Reuben's dream to reach them all with radio. He talks about hanging 'singing radios' from bamboo trees out in the jungle. Can you imagine the impact that coming across a radio booming out Christian songs in their own language would have on the Indians."

"Yes, I can," Clarence replied, his heart beating fast. "How do you think the Ecuadorian government would feel about issuing a radio license to a Protestant organization?"

"I'm not sure," Grace said, taking another sip of her milk shake. "In some ways Ecuador is the most progressive country in South America. It had the first university and the first hospital. I suppose it could have the first radio station on the continent as well. Wouldn't it be wonderful if it were a Christian one?"

"Yes, it would," Clarence replied, feeling hope rising in his heart but hardly daring to trust his feelings. The last thing he wanted was another faith-sapping adventure.

As the conversation wound down, Clarence invited the Larson family to stay with them when they came to speak in Chicago.

It was another month before the Larsons were due to arrive in Chicago, and during that time Clarence often found himself wondering whether the injunction to go south with radio was finally about to become a reality.

Finally, in January 1930, Reuben and Grace Larson, along with their two children, Dick and Peggy, arrived to stay with the Joneses in their apartment. Soon after the Larsons' arrival, Katherine invited the Clark family to join them all for dinner one evening, and soon the children were having a riotous time together. While they jumped on beds and slid down the arms of the sofa, the six adults were in deep conversation.

The hours ticked by as Clarence told of his leading to start a radio station in South America and how frustrated he had become when things did not work out. The Larsons and the Clarks explained what they knew of how the government of Ecuador worked, and at 3:00 AM they all prayed together.

By now the children had fallen asleep on the floor, and the room was quiet except for their prayers. "Lord, we pledge ourselves to bring to reality the vision of missionary broadcasting. Go before us, Lord, and open the way," Clarence prayed.

Now that they had pledged themselves to making Christian radio a reality in South America, each man took on a role. Since Reuben already enjoyed a good relationship with the government of Ecuador, he volunteered to work on gaining a permit from the government for such a venture. He planned to start as soon as his furlough was over. Clarence and John agreed to join ranks at home and raise money and spread the word about the new endeavor.

Over the next several days, the three men hammered out in writing the aims and purposes of the radio station to present to the government. As Clarence thought back over his previous experiences trying to persuade South American governments to give him a radio license, he realized that the time he had spent visiting South America had not been wasted after all. He had gained useful insight into the government officials' fears, and now as they wrote, he did all he could to allay them.

The men promised that the radio station would always send a positive, hopeful message and that it would not promote any one denomination or comment on political situations. It would also offer the government radio time to broadcast farming advice, weather reports, and cultural programs. In exchange the men asked that the government lift the tariffs on all of the radio equipment they would need to import and allow long-term visas for radio workers.

The document the three men wrote with the president of Ecuador in mind stated in part:

> We desire to present this offer to your esteemed President and the people of Ecuador....
>
> We desire to join forces with Mr. Larson and his associates for a larger and more efficient spreading of the Gospel in Ecuador by

means of a radio broadcasting station to be erected, with your permission, by us at Quito or some satisfactory place.

While we desire to install this station primarily for Gospel purposes, there are other advantages that will come through it to Ecuador. Here are a few.... It will pioneer the way for later systems of communication.... It will open vast sections of Ecuador's interior to world news and happenings.... It will allow for regular instruction classes in the language and history of Ecuador to educate the poorer classes in the villages and inaccessible mountain districts.... It will allow broadcasting of the Presidential messages.... Most important of all, it will at once bring Ecuador further into the march of world progress which other South American governments have already entered....

We propose to carry out, with your permission, the following plan for Gospel radio broadcasting in Ecuador...to erect a modern, thoroughly equipped radio broadcasting transmitter for Gospel broadcasting; and to place receiving sets (free of cost) at convenient places throughout the country to receive the Gospel messages we broadcast....

May we remind you that our whole objective in presenting this offer is the unselfish motive of every true Missionary who desires to further the Gospel of the Lord Jesus Christ, and the blessing of Ecuador, spiritually and economically.

Excited by the prospects of what lay ahead, Clarence could hardly wait to tell everyone at the Chicago Gospel Tabernacle about their intentions. When he did, to his surprise, the plan received a mixed reception. By now most Christians at the tabernacle had adjusted to the idea that radio could be used for godly means, but the idea of using it on the foreign mission field was still laughed at. Some in the congregation called the idea "Jones's folly" and pointed out that Reuben Larson had said that there were only six radio receivers in the whole of Ecuador. Even Paul Rader's sister was skeptical. "What's the point of sending out a radio message if no one can receive it. It's like putting gasoline stations in a country where there are no cars," she said.

Clarence had thought about that too, but it was a case of which came first, the chicken or the egg. Until there was a radio station in the country, there was no reason for anyone to own a radio. Yet if a radio station were set up, there was no equipment to hear it on.

Other people, including Clarence's brother-in-law Chet, were concerned about the timing of the whole venture. After the Wall Street crash in October 1929, the United States was in financial turmoil. Unemployment rose every day, and interest rates were making it impossible for those with jobs to stay in their own homes. It was not a good time to start a new mission, especially one that needed expensive equipment.

Clarence had one answer for those who doubted whether he was doing the right thing or not. "What you are saying might be exactly right, but when you start a work of this kind, everything is an obstacle. And the more obstacles you have, the more opportunities there are for God to do something."

Clarence knew it seemed foolhardy from a human standpoint, but he also knew that people had laughed at Paul Rader when he began his radio ministry just eight years before. "Although it seems like poor timing," he told people, "we believe it's God's timing, and we will press ahead."

The next obstacle for the men to overcome was to gain permission from the Christian and Missionary Alliance (CMA), under whose auspices Reuben Larson and John Clark served, to move ahead with their plans. The leader of the Christian and Missionary Alliance was Dr. Walter Turnbull. Clarence had met Dr. Turnbull several times, since Paul was very active in the CMA movement. Clarence, Reuben, and John set out for Pittsburgh, where the CMA was holding its annual conference. The three men were tense as they met with Dr. Turnbull. If he did not see the potential of radio in South America and did not give his blessing to the project, they could not go on with it together.

Dr. Turnbull put the three young men at ease right away. "Yes, yes," he beamed, "radio is full of possibilities. We must think in broad strokes here.

To reach the world with the gospel of Jesus Christ, we need strong transmitters in three locations. I have given it some thought myself, and I believe we need one in the Philippines for Asia, one somewhere in South America for the millions of Spanish and Portuguese speakers, and one in Palestine for Africa and the Moslem world."

The three men nodded. Dr. Turnbull continued, warming even more to his subject. "If you can get into South America and launch gospel radio from there, go for it!"

Clarence, Reuben, and John were elated by Dr. Turnbull's response. Now they could move ahead with the project at full speed. In fact, the Larsons were heading back to Ecuador at the end of the conference, and Reuben promised to present the proposal to the Ecuadorian government as soon as he arrived in Quito.

At the conference Clarence was introduced to Paul Young. Paul was one of the earliest CMA missionaries, having gone to serve in Ecuador in 1919. He had arrived from Ecuador to attend the conference, and when he learned what Clarence, Reuben, and John were planning, he became very excited. Paul was passionate about sharing the gospel with as many people as possible in his lifetime, and he immediately saw how radio could help to exponentially increase the number of people who could hear the gospel at one time. Paul lent his support to the project and offered to help the three young men in any way he could once he got back to Ecuador.

Clarence said good-bye to Reuben and Grace and left the conference brimming with faith and enthusiasm. Sure, there would be challenges ahead, but with God's blessing, they would overcome them all.

Before returning to Chicago, Clarence decided to take the train to Washington, D.C. He had heard that the U.S. State Department had done some research on good places to locate radio transmitters in Central and South America, and he was eager to hear where they thought the best place in Ecuador would be.

It was a hot, humid day in Washington as Clarence made his way along Pennsylvania Avenue. Clarence thought about how well everything was falling into place as he padded his way up the steps and entered the imposing Department of State building. Inside the building the temperature was almost chilly as he made his way down a corridor to the reception area.

"I would like to see a secretary in the South American division," Clarence told the middle-aged man with graying hair who sat behind the information desk.

"And whom shall I say is calling, sir?" the man asked.

"Jones. Clarence Jones," Clarence replied.

Several minutes later Clarence was led down another corridor and into a large, airy office. A well-dressed official shook Clarence's hand and invited him to sit down in one of the chairs beside the desk. "I understand you want to know about radio in

South America," the official began. "How can I help you?"

"I understand that this department has gathered a considerable amount of data on radio broadcasting experience and problems around the world. Do you have much on South America?" Clarence inquired.

"We have some, especially on the larger countries like Mexico, Brazil, and Argentina," the official replied.

"And what about Ecuador?" Clarence asked.

"We don't have much on Ecuador. There's no radio there," the official said, rising from his chair and walking over to a file cabinet from which he pulled a brown folder. "This is all we have," he said as he took his seat again. He opened the folder and turned it so that Clarence could see. "As you can see, reception conditions there are just about nil."

"But if a radio station were to be built in Ecuador, where do you think is the best spot to put it?" Clarence asked.

The official picked up the folder and scanned it before he answered. "I would definitely not put up a radio station in Ecuador at all," he replied. "Get as far away from the equator as you can. Try some other country down there, but keep away from the equator," the official repeated for emphasis.

Clarence sat stunned for a moment. The equator went right through Ecuador—that was how the country got its name. And Quito, the capital city, where they planned to build the radio station, sat high in the mountains on the equator. Finally Clarence could not think of anything else to say, so he thanked the official for his time and left.

As he walked out of the State Department building into the stifling afternoon and made his way back down Pennsylvania Avenue, the words of the State Department official rang in his ears: "Try some other country down there, but keep away from the equator." These were not the words Clarence had been expecting to hear. What should he make of them?

Chapter 7

Ecuador at Last

Several weeks later Clarence was still pondering the warning of the State Department official when he received a letter from Ecuador, from Reuben Larson. He eagerly tore open the envelope and read. Reuben reported that things were going well. He had described to Stuart Clark the plan to establish a Christian radio station in the country. Stuart was John Clark's brother and served as the field director for the Christian and Missionary Alliance in Ecuador. He was excited by the prospect of a radio station and had offered to throw his energy and influence into helping Reuben win approval from the government for the project. Reuben reported that the initial meetings between him and Stuart and government representatives had been favorable and that they believed it would not be too long before approval for the project was given.

As he read, Clarence could not help but wonder what was going wrong at home. God seemed to be moving all sorts of obstacles in Quito so that the plan to establish a radio station would get a fair hearing before the government. But in the United States everyone who knew anything about radio thought it was a terrible idea to locate a radio transmitting station in Quito. Clarence did not know what to think, and over the next few weeks the gap between what was happening at home and the wonderful breakthroughs in Quito widened.

Several days later Clarence received another letter from Reuben. Reuben reported that the president's secretary was willing to push for the radio station, even though the secretary had confided in Reuben that as a strong Catholic, he thought it should be his duty to oppose a Protestant venture such as this one.

This was enough for Clarence. Although he did not understand why God was leading them to set up a radio station in a place everyone seemed to object to, he decided to move ahead with the plan anyway. He encouraged himself with the words from Hebrews 11:1: "Now faith is the substance of things hoped for, the evidence of things not seen." Clarence had to admit that things did not make sense, but he decided to advance in faith. He booked passage aboard the *Santa Inez* for August 20, 1930.

This was the same ship that John and Ruth Clark were returning to Ecuador aboard following their furlough. Clarence figured that they could use the twelve days of the voyage to continue planning for the radio station.

This gave Clarence only three weeks to get ready for the trip and to talk about the project with as many people as possible. When he told Katherine of his plans, she gasped and flopped into the nearest chair. She was silent for several minutes, and then she seemed to collect herself. "In that case," she told Clarence, "you are going to need all the help you can get. I'll leave the girls with Ruth and Chet, and we'd better get started. We have a lot of people to see before you sail."

At that moment, more than at any other, Clarence was grateful for his wife's faith in the project. Katherine was right: he did need all the help he could get.

The two of them set out on a whirlwind tour from Chicago to New York. They had intended to go north to Canada, but their car broke down several times, and they had to change their plans. The twelve years under Paul Rader's ministry had brought Clarence into contact with many prominent church leaders from a number of denominations, and now he contacted as many of those leaders as possible. When he asked to speak to them and their congregations about the vision of a radio ministry in South America, he received a variety of responses. Some pastors arranged special meetings and opened their pulpits for Clarence to speak. Others were more skeptical and put off meeting with Clarence, saying that their congregations were not yet ready to think about using such a new technology as a missionary tool.

Clarence and Katherine spoke wherever and whenever they could, and to their surprise, many people began to take an interest in seeing a radio station established in Ecuador.

When Clarence arrived in New York, he learned that the *Santa Inez* would be sailing a day early, on August 19. He went straight to the Ecuadorian consulate to secure a visa for his trip. On August 15, while he was still in New York City, he received a cable from Reuben that read, "25-year contract granted! Jeremiah 33:3 and Zechariah 4:6! Come!"

Clarence could scarcely believe it. The Ecuadorian government had granted them a contract to establish and run a Christian radio station in their country. He pulled out his leather-bound Bible and looked up the two verses Reuben had alluded to in the cable. "Call unto me, and I will answer thee, and shew thee great and mighty things, which thou knowest not" (Jeremiah 33:3). "Not by might, nor by power, but by my spirit, saith the LORD of hosts" (Zechariah 4:6). Clarence bowed his head and said a prayer of thanks to God. Indeed, it had not been their might or power or diplomacy or anything else that had secured the contract to run the radio station. It had been God working on the hearts of men in Ecuador on their behalf that had brought it to pass. When he had finished praying, Clarence laid aside his Bible and went off to tell Katherine the good news.

With his visa in hand, Clarence realized that he had just enough time to head to Massachusetts to visit Richard Oliver Jr. Richard was in Dudley, sixty miles southwest of Boston. Clarence had already asked Richard to move to Ecuador once the radio station was established and head up the musical side of things for the radio broadcasts. Initially Richard had wanted to accompany Clarence on this trip, but it had not worked out financially for him to go along.

Excitedly Clarence showed Richard the cable he had received from Reuben, and the two of them rejoiced. Then the two men climbed into the car and headed for Boston, where they played on the *Mountain Top Hour* radio broadcast from WEAN.

At lunchtime on August 19, 1930, Clarence stood at the rail of the *Santa Inez,* waving to Katherine as a tugboat pulled the ship away from the pier in Brooklyn. Soon the vessel passed through the Verrazano Narrows, at the entrance to New York Harbor, and headed out to sea. It headed south down the east coast of the United States before turning west and heading for Panama, where it passed through the Panama Canal into the Pacific Ocean. The *Santa Inez* then steamed south along the west coast of South America before finally reaching Guayaquil, Ecuador's main port. Throughout the voyage Clarence and John and Ruth Clark talked excitedly about all that lay ahead with the radio station now that they had been granted a twenty-five-year contract.

From the moment he saw Guayaquil from the deck of the *Santa Inez,* anchored in the Guayas River, Clarence liked the place. The river was alive with small boats and balsa wood rafts loaded with enormous stalks of bananas or mounds of coconuts headed for the market. Overcrowded ferry boats carried people from one side of the river to the other, while large barges ferried crates of cargo ashore from the freighters anchored in the river or farther downstream in the Gulf of Guayaquil. The edge of the river was lined with palm trees drooping in the languid afternoon heat. Small huts and shacks were scattered along the river's edge, where there were no docks. And stretched out beyond the docks and the palm trees were the streets and buildings of Guayaquil, alive with people and cars and activity.

Finally, after clearing customs and immigration and being ferried ashore in a small launch, Clarence stepped onto Ecuadorian soil. It was as though electricity pulsed through him at that moment. After his negative experience in Venezuela, he was excited to know that the government of this country had already given its permission for a radio station. Now Clarence and his partners had to make it happen!

Waiting at the dock in Guayaquil to meet Clarence and the Clarks was Paul Young, who was full of excitement for the future of radio broadcasting in Ecuador.

The following day John and Ruth Clark and their children set out for Quito and then on to Ambato to resume their missionary duties. Once they had left, Clarence sat down, pulled a fountain pen and several sheets of paper from his leather satchel and wrote a letter to Katherine.

Sunday, August 31, 1930

Dearest Sweetheart,

At last we have arrived in Ecuador. Our boat docked yesterday at about 4:00 PM, and Mr. Young with several other missionaries met us....

Our steamer had to anchor in mid stream, and our luggage, with us, was taken off by launches. The tide—a very swift one here—was running out, so we had quite a thrilling journey to shore, about a mile away.

Guayaquil is by far the biggest and nicest South American city I have seen so far. I expect we'll stay here a week and then move on up to Quito to see Stuart Clark. Reuben has gone back into the jungle and will not be out until the Field Conference to be held Oct. 3 to 9. This means I will probably have to go into the jungle to see him, first, so I can hurry things along and get back to you.

Boy, oh, boy! How I miss you, honey. If there weren't so many missionaries around and so much to do—I would mind this lonesomeness much more....

God is moving in a marvelous way down here. I have not seen such open-hearted attention to the gospel anywhere before....

> There seems to be every opportunity in the world to get out the gospel here. I only hope the radio project proves sufficiently practical from what I find out here to be used of the Lord for souls. I can see an increasing need for us all to know the language well....
>
> Tonite, I am to bring the message; there will be between 200 and 300 present. I know you will be praying, darling. I remember you all each morning and evening.

Clarence was kept busy during his week in Guayaquil. Every day he was up early and on his way to speak and play his trombone at various church meetings in Guayaquil and some of the outlying small towns. During this time Clarence, who always liked to be on time, found one aspect of living in Ecuador very frustrating. Nothing seemed to run on schedule. Clarence would arrive at the railway station with Paul Young to travel to an outlying town, only to find that the train had left early or had been cancelled or was running two hours behind schedule. And, of course, getting to the railway station was equally as frustrating. The railway station was located across the Guayas River from the city, and to get there required a ferry boat ride. But like the trains, ferry boats were either early, late, or canceled. On more than one occasion Clarence found himself riding on horseback to get to a meeting venue because of the unreliability of the train and ferry boat schedules. Describing the situation in his journal, Clarence wrote, "This is the land of mañana for sure. The auto truck we are to take at 7:00 AM does not get away until 9:30.... We've missed two trains lately, so not to be fooled today, we arrive at 4:00 AM to catch the 4:30 train. It finally pulls in at 5:15, and doesn't leave till after 6:00."

One of the last things Clarence purchased for the journey before setting sail from New York City was a 16-millimeter movie camera. Clarence had decided that with so many questions about the notion of using radio as a missionary tool, it might be a good idea to film some of the opportunities that existed for using Christian radio in Ecuador. Everywhere he went throughout Guayaquil and the surrounding countryside, Clarence had the movie camera at the ready to catch any interesting or unusual footage that might offer people back home some insight into the life and culture of Ecuador.

One humid evening in Guayaquil, as Clarence sat in a small, open-air café, he heard the sound of American voices floating through the air. He looked around. The voices belonged to two men sitting in a far corner of the café. Clarence walked over to the men and introduced himself. The men invited him to join them, and they struck up a conversation. To Clarence's amazement the two men were radio engineers. They had been sent to Ecuador by the manufacturer of radio receivers to research the possibility of setting up a radio broadcasting station in

Ecuador. It seemed to Clarence as though God had set up the meeting between them. "And what have you discovered?" he eagerly asked them.

"There's no way it can be done here," they told him. "Ecuador has too many mountains. And the high mineral content of the rock, with its strong magnetic force, will seriously weaken, absorb, or hopelessly scramble any signal. Whatever you do, stay away from the mountains!"

Clarence's heart began to sink. This was not what he had hoped to hear. He thought back to Washington, D.C., and the State Department official's telling him that radio reception in Ecuador was just about nil. "I would definitely not put up a radio station in Ecuador at all. You must get as far away from the equator as you can," the official had said. And now here were two radio engineers telling him the same thing. But Clarence and the others now had a contract with the government to set up a radio station in Ecuador.

Later that night as Clarence strolled along the Guayas River, he pondered the situation. The plan was to establish the radio station in Quito. But Quito was situated 9,300 feet above sea level in the Andes Mountains. And as if that were not enough, it lay just ten miles south of the equator. These were the two things the two radio engineers at the café and the official in Washington had warned him to stay away from. Perhaps, Clarence wondered, they should situate the radio station here in Guayaquil. After all, the city was sited away from the mountains at sea level, it was Ecuador's main port and commercial center, and it had a number of thriving Protestant churches. Situating the radio station in Guayaquil certainly made a lot of sense.

Even as he thought these things, Clarence was aware of another voice in his head saying, "Come up to the top of the mountain." He recognized the words as those that God had spoken to Moses in the Old Testament.

"Come up to the top of the mountain? When all the engineers are telling us we're crazy to even be in Ecuador, let alone in Quito. Is this what You are really saying, Lord?" Clarence questioned.

"Come up to the top of the mountain. Call unto Me, and I will show you great and mighty things," the voice echoed in his head. Clarence recognized the words of the last sentence. They were from Jeremiah 33:3, one of the verses Reuben Larson had referenced when he sent the telegram informing Clarence that a twenty-five-year contract to run a radio station had been approved by the government. And hadn't the other verse Reuben referenced, Zechariah 4:6, said, "Not by might, nor by power, but by my spirit, saith the Lord of hosts."

It might seem crazy and illogical, given what the radio engineers and State Department official had told him, but Clarence was certain that they were supposed to establish the radio station in Quito, high in the mountains. No matter what people thought, he, Clarence Jones, was going up to the top of the mountain in obedience to God's command. Of course the other men involved in the project would have to agree. But for Clarence the matter was settled.

Convinced that God was going to bless their venture, Clarence pressed ahead with his plan. Before leaving Guayaquil he met with the Reed brothers. John and Alan Reed were the sons of William Reed, one of the first Protestant missionaries to arrive in Ecuador, in 1898. The brothers ran a stationery business in Guayaquil, and they agreed that if a radio station were established that broadcast to the nation, they would import and sell radio receivers throughout Ecuador.

With the agreement made, Clarence headed for the railway station and the train to Quito.

Chapter 8

Up to the Mountains

To Clarence's surprise the train for the two-day journey to Quito departed almost on time. As it chugged away from Guayaquil, Clarence was able to get a good look at the country that he was planning to make home. For the first few hours of the journey, palm trees and a tropical forest grew up to the edge of the railway line. But slowly, as the narrow-gauge train began to climb up from sea level, the tropical forest gave way to mountain vistas with waterfalls cascading from bare, rocky heights, filling the air with a rainbow of spray. As usual, Clarence had his movie camera at the ready to capture the beauty of the landscape. When the train began its ascent of the Andes Mountains, he found himself leaning out the window with the camera.

The climb up the Andes was an amazing experience. The ledge on which the train tracks rested had been chiseled from the rock face. The train inched its way along the track, climbing steeply as it did so. Then it came to a stop on a siding. A guard climbed off the train, pulled a lever, and switched the points. The train then began moving again, this time backing up along the next stretch of track until coming to rest on another siding. The points were switched again, and the train moved forward up the next length of track. Slowly the train began to zigzag its way up the rock face. In fifty miles of switching backward and forward in this manner, the train climbed ten thousand feet up into the mountains. And as the train moved along, Clarence filmed the sheer drop from the train to the valley floor far below.

Leaving the switchbacks behind, the train chugged even higher into the mountains, traveling across a cold, desolate plateau where few people lived. It steamed past Mount Chimborazo, a snow-capped volcano and the highest point in Ecuador, reaching to a height of 20,709 feet above sea level. Finally the train climbed through the cloud line, where it rumbled along above the clouds. Once again Clarence had the movie camera outside the window, filming the clouds below.

Eventually they reached a height of 11,800 feet before the narrow-gauge train began its descent into Quito. Clarence was glad that they did not go any higher, because at that altitude, the air was thin, and he found himself gasping for air, especially when he tried to move around. By the time the train pulled into the station in Quito, Clarence had experienced the most exciting and the most scenic rail journey of his life.

Waiting to meet Clarence at the station in Quito was Stuart Clark. It was the first time the two men had met, and Clarence liked Stuart right away. Stuart was a gracious and charming person who welcomed Clarence to Quito. As Stuart led the way through the streets of Quito, Clarence could see for himself what a city of contrasts the place was. Quito was the oldest capital in South America, and its maze of narrow streets was lined with old stone churches and buildings, some of which, Stuart pointed out, were over three hundred years old. But Quito was also a modern city. It had broad, tree-lined avenues, along which gleaming new buildings had been erected. Beyond the broad avenues and narrow streets, the city was surrounded by soaring, rocky, snowcapped mountain peaks that reached high into the thin, clear-blue atmosphere.

That evening Clarence ate dinner with Stuart and his American wife, Erma. As they ate, Stuart filled Clarence in on the details of how the government had decided to grant them a license to establish a radio station.

"My office is located right across the street from the government's lawyer," Stuart began. "One day when I saw him leaving his office, I raced outside, where I managed to meet the man. His name is Dr.

Luís Calisto. He is a wonderful man, and we became friends. He has a very favorable view of the work done in Ecuador by missionaries, and when I mentioned to him our desire to start a radio station in his country, he became very excited."

"That's wonderful," Clarence commented while Stuart stopped to take a bite of food.

"Yes," Stuart said, taking up the story again. "Dr. Calisto was the man who worked out all the final details of the contract, and he was very fair and thorough. But God moved a lot of hearts along the way before Dr. Calisto was able to do his part. Reuben and I submitted the proposal for the radio station to the government official who presents such things to Congress and the president. But this man was troubled by the proposal. 'How can I approve the establishing of a Protestant radio station in a Catholic country?' he asked himself, and he set the proposal aside.

"In the meantime Reuben and I waited patiently and prayed much about the proposal, asking God to grant us favor with the government. Finally the official to whom we had submitted the proposal decided to read through it again. He was still conflicted about a Protestant radio station in a Catholic country, but as he told me later, 'There was something inside me that impelled me to put my signature on the document.' And with that the gentleman signed the front of the proposal, stamped '*visto bueno*' (approved) on it, and sent it on to the president's office."

"Where God's finger points, God's hand will open the door," Clarence said, as Erma Clark reached over and took his now empty plate.

"Quite so," Stuart said, "but there's more to the story. At the president's office, his young clerk, Carlos Andrade Marín, saw the proposal for a radio station in Ecuador and became very excited. He put the proposal at the top of a pile of papers awaiting the president's attention. But the next morning he found that it had been moved to the bottom of the pile. So he pulled it out and once again placed it on top. He had to do this several times before the president finally looked at the proposal. The president was impressed enough to send it on to Congress to be voted on. Congress voted and approved the proposal, and Luís Calisto was asked to draw up a contract, which he did, and the president signed it. So now, here we are, ready to take the next step."

"Indeed we are," Clarence said, trying not to think of the gloomy warning the radio engineers had given him in Guayaquil several days before.

The following day Clarence was out exploring Quito some more. "Quito, this ancient, glorious capital of Ecuador, is a great city. I like its people, its beauty, its progressive air. The climate is wonderfully fresh and invigorating," he wrote in his journal later that day.

Clarence had been disappointed to learn on his arrival in Quito that Reuben and Grace Larson had returned to their mission station at Dos Ríos in the Oriente. He was anxious to see the couple again, and so, several days after arriving in Quito, Clarence set out with Stuart to visit the Larsons.

"Dos Ríos is only seventy-five miles away as the crow flies," Stuart informed Clarence, "but to get there overland is an arduous journey. It will take us two days on horseback, another three days of hiking, and then another day or two on horseback."

On the day of their departure, Clarence and Stuart were up a 1:30 AM. They ate a hearty breakfast and were then driven by car two hours south of Quito to the trailhead, where a local Indian guide met them. Since the trail they would be following passed through a desolate and largely uninhabited area, they had to carry with them all the supplies they would need for the journey. Once these supplies were loaded onto two packhorses, Clarence and Stuart mounted their horses, and they were off. It was still two hours before dawn, and their guide, walking ahead in the silvery moonlight, led the way. At 6:00 AM the sun finally emerged and turned the snowcapped mountain peaks into mounds of glistening gold.

With the sun up, Clarence could finally see for himself just how desolate and uninhabited the land was. Snow lay on the ground, and soon after sunrise a cold, drenching rain began to fall. Clarence was glad that he had brought along a rubber poncho, which he pulled over his head to protect himself against the elements.

The Indian guide led the men across a broad plateau between two rows of mountain peaks.

By midafternoon, Clarence, who was still getting accustomed to the altitude of Quito, found himself getting light-headed and gasping for air. That was when Stuart informed him that they had climbed to an altitude of 13,500 feet above sea level. The good news was that this was as high as they would climb and that before they made camp for the night, they would have already begun their descent down the other side of the Andes. Sure enough, by the time they stopped for the night and had set up camp in the shelter of a rocky outcrop, Clarence was again breathing easier, and he no longer felt so light-headed.

Despite how he felt, Clarence always had his movie camera at the ready to capture on film as much of the experience as he could.

After a chilly night bundled under a pile of blankets by the fire, the group set out again the next morning. Once again the Indian guide walked ahead on foot, leading the two packhorses. Throughout the day the men continued their descent of the eastern side of the Andes Mountains. The trail they followed was rough and steep and in many places had been washed away by landslides, causing the men to make numerous detours. By early afternoon Clarence was noticing more and more trees dotting the barren landscape, and by late afternoon the group had descended into dense jungle. They were now in the Oriente, the eastern portion of Ecuador that was the headwaters of the mighty Amazon River, which flowed eastward for two thousand miles to the sea.

As the sun began to set and they stopped to set up camp for the night, Clarence noted the change in climate. The night before he had shivered under a pile of blankets, trying to keep warm; now, in the damp, tropical air of the Oriente, he barely needed a blanket.

The following morning it was time to leave the horses behind and set out on foot through the jungle. Three more Indians arrived at the camp in the morning, to carry the supplies that had been on the packhorses. Once the supplies were loaded onto the Indians' backs, the group was off through the jungle. By now Clarence was glad to be walking. After two days on horseback, he was stiff and saddle sore. It did not take him too long, however, to discover that this part of the journey was going to be far more difficult and physically taxing than riding on horseback over the Andes.

The trail wound up and over ridge after ridge of foothills, across streams and rivers, and through dense jungle. And if that were not difficult enough, Clarence found himself clambering over the moss-covered trunks of massive, fallen trees. He was amazed at the agile way the Indians slid over the tree trunks, while it required so much effort for him to pull himself over them.

As the day wore on, Clarence found his energy slipping away fast. He was falling behind the others, and eventually Stuart fell back to help and encourage him on. Finally, when the Indians had gotten so far ahead that they were almost out of view, Stuart yelled for them to wait. Since Clarence was too exhausted to continue, Stuart instructed the Indians to construct a small shelter for them for the night. Using bamboo and leaves, the Indians followed his orders, and soon a dome-shaped structure was nestled beside the trail. After eating some dinner, Clarence crawled inside and fell fast asleep. He was too exhausted to care that the floor of the small shelter was mostly mud that squelched under him.

The following morning Clarence emerged from the shelter bleary-eyed but well rested, and much to his delight, his strength had returned. After a cup of coffee and some breakfast, they broke camp and set out again. This time, though, Stuart had told the Indians to slow their pace, and Clarence found it much easier to keep up. However, traveling at a slower pace meant it took them five days to cover what was normally covered in three days. And when they finally switched back to horses for the final two days of the journey, Clarence could not have been happier. He decided that feeling stiff and saddle sore was a small price to pay for not having to slog on foot through the dense jungle.

Finally, nine days after setting out from Quito, they arrived at Dos Ríos. Much to Clarence's dismay, however, Reuben and Grace Larson were not there. The couple had left two days before for Quito, following the longer but less arduous route over the mountains through the towns of Baños and Ambato, to attend the annual Missionary Alliance Conference. Despite the Larsons' absence, Clarence and Stuart spent two days exploring the area around Dos Ríos in dugout canoes.

After two days of observing jungle life among the Quichua Indians around Dos Ríos, Clarence and Stuart set out for Quito the way they had come. They, too, had to get back for the annual Missionary Alliance Conference, where Clarence was scheduled to lead the music. For some reason Clarence found the journey back much less stressful, though it was punctuated with numerous stops for him to set up his movie camera and film expansive vistas of the Oriente.

When he arrived safely back in Quito, Clarence could not help but wonder how much easier the whole trip to Dos Ríos would have been in an airplane. In just one hour of flying they could have crossed the same terrain that took them nine days to cross on horseback and by foot.

Back in Quito, Clarence was finally reunited with Reuben and Grace Larson, John and Ruth Clark, and Paul Young and his wife, Bernice, who were all attending the annual Missionary Alliance Conference in the city. It was a wonderful reunion, and as the conference progressed, they all got together to talk about the next step in setting up the radio station. Clarence felt that he had to tell the others about meeting the radio engineers in Guayaquil and about their warning to stay away from the mountains. But as the group prayed about the matter, they all agreed that God was directing them to establish the new radio station in Quito despite the warnings they had received. With that matter settled, they moved on to talk about what to call the station.

"So what are we going to call this new radio station?" Clarence asked,

"By international agreement, each country is assigned a call letter or letters that identify where the station originates from," Stuart began. "In the United States, those call letters are *K* and *W*. The call letters of every radio station there must start with one of those letters, as you well know, Clarence. Here in Ecuador the call letters for the country are *HC*. Whatever call sign we come up with for the station, it must start with *HC*, to which we can add two more letters."

"Back in Chicago we used the slogan 'Where Jesus Blesses Thousands' to come up with the call letters for station WJBT. Do you think we could come up with a similar slogan for our new call sign?" Clarence asked.

"That's a good idea, but it must be in Spanish, since most of our programming will be," John said.

"How about *Hoy Cristo*?" Stuart suggested.

Everyone nodded and then Reuben Larson chimed in, "*Hoy Cristo Jesús Bendice*" (Today Jesus Christ Blesses).

"It has a nice ring to it," Clarence said, while the other men nodded approvingly. "Then that will be it, and the call letters will be HCJB."

"Do you think we could come up with a slogan using those letters in English as well?" John asked.

This challenge proved a little more difficult, but eventually they came up with a slogan in English that they all liked—"Heralding Christ Jesus' Blessings."

Following the annual Missionary Alliance Conference, Clarence spent the remainder of his time in Quito searching for a site for the new radio station. But as hard as he looked, he could not find a suitable site. While he was searching for the site, Clarence was praying fervently that God would somehow provide the six hundred dollars he needed to make the return trip to the United States. Clarence also expressed his need to the group, and miraculously, Reuben had recently received six hundred dollars. This was a large amount of money for a missionary to have, and Reuben offered to loan it to Clarence so that he could buy a ticket home. Clarence accepted the offer and booked passage back to the United States.

Chapter 9

Trials and Tribulations

As he stepped aboard the steamer in Guayaquil on October 20, 1930, Clarence knew that there were many challenges ahead. Yet, as the ship left Ecuador behind, he was optimistic about the future. In just two weeks he would be back in Chicago, juggling his job at the Chicago Gospel Tabernacle with raising awareness and money for the new radio station HCJB. Or at least that was what Clarence thought he would be doing. But when the steamer docked at New York City, bad news awaited him.

While Clarence had been at sea, steaming his way back from Ecuador, his best friend, Richard Oliver Jr., had been killed in a car accident. The funeral had already been held, and all Clarence could do was to visit his friend's grave and mourn for him there. It was a bitter blow. Clarence had been sure that

Richard would play a prominent role in HCJB, but now Richard was gone, and it was not to be.

Clarence returned to Chicago in a somber mood, only to be met with still more bad news. A letter waiting at the apartment informed Clarence that his employment at the Chicago Gospel Tabernacle had been terminated and his job given to someone else in his absence. To add insult to injury, there was also a bill for the two thousand dollars of tabernacle money he had used for passage to Ecuador and to support the family while he had been away.

It was hard for Clarence to take in all these changes. His best friend was dead, he had been fired from his job, he was flat broke, and on top of the six hundred dollars he owed Reuben Larson for his passage home, he now owed the Chicago Gospel Tabernacle the enormous sum of two thousand dollars. And all this at the same time he was supposed to be launching the new radio station. Things had never looked so grim.

The day after arriving back in Chicago, Clarence visited Paul Rader. Paul informed him that in his absence a very conservative church missions director had been appointed, and the new director was behind both the firing and the bill. The new missions director apparently did not believe that radio had a role to play in missionary work. And while Paul sympathized with Clarence's plight, he did not want to interfere with the missions director's decision, especially since the deepening economic depression meant that giving was down and money was in short supply at the church. Paul explained that the man was trying to do the best for the Chicago Gospel Tabernacle with what he had.

Clarence returned to the family's apartment feeling even more depressed. It seemed so unfair that one man could cause him so much heartache. There did not appear to be any way through his problems. As he thought about what to do next, Clarence found himself repeating his favorite Bible verses over and over to himself. And as he repeated Jeremiah 33:3, "Call unto me, and I will answer thee, and shew thee great and mighty things," he began to draw strength from it.

The following day Clarence decided to disclose his desperate situation to others, and the all-night prayer group that met at the tabernacle offered to pray that night for the Jones family.

The next day Clarence received a phone call from an old friend, Dr. Gerald Winrod. Gerald explained that he had moved to Oklahoma City and opened a new Gospel Tabernacle there. He was modeling the new tabernacle on the one in Chicago and needed someone to help with the radio ministry. In response Clarence told Gerald that his heart was in Ecuador and that he planned to move to Quito as soon as he could raise the money needed to start a radio station there.

Much to Clarence's surprise, this did not dint Gerald's enthusiasm. Gerald still wanted Clarence to help with the radio ministry. "Come as soon as you can," he said, "and what you learn here with the radio ministry will help you when you get to the mission field. I also have some ideas on ways to help you get the money you need." That was all the encouragement Clarence needed, and he and his family were soon on their way to Oklahoma City.

By now it was nearly Christmas, and upon his arrival in Oklahoma City, Clarence found himself immersed in running the festive music program. Once 1931 arrived, however, he had more time on his hands, and Gerald encouraged him to press on with the radio project. To help him along, Gerald invited Clarence to take a seat on the board of his magazine, which was called the *Defender*. This magazine had a huge Christian readership, and Clarence was permitted to write articles about his plans for a radio station in Ecuador. In one lead article in the *Defender*, Clarence laid out his plan of action.

> Our whole creed of service is "Use everything we can that God has given us in this Twentieth Century to speed the taking of the First Century Message." Thus we restate Paul's challenge: "By all means save some."…
>
> Thank God for the many advanced methods that today are at the missionary's disposal. Radio Station HCJB, with its 5000 watts on shortwave, is in itself a most revolutionary step forward in missionary endeavor. This step calls for kindred steps all along the line as we seek to develop the many possibilities before us.

By "kindred steps" Clarence meant that he was looking for others who shared a vision similar to his and were willing to explore the possibilities of radio evangelism with him. Sure enough, letters and phone calls began to pour in as a result of the article. People from all over the United States wanted to know how they could get involved in the project.

In March 1931 Clarence, Katherine, and the children took time off to visit Katherine's father in Lima, Ohio. Katherine's Uncle Ben was visiting there as well, and the three men began talking about the new radio station. Ben Welty, a lawyer and former congressman, encouraged Clarence to form a legal corporation before he accepted any more donations. The advice made sense to Clarence, and he started thinking about a name that would be suitable for many types of radio ministries around the world. He came up with the name "World Radio Missionary Fellowship," or WRMF for short. The new organization was incorporated on March 9, with Clarence as president, his father-in-law as treasurer, Katherine's sister Ruth as secretary, and Lance and Virginia Latham from the Chicago Gospel Tabernacle, Clarence's brother Howard Jones, and Reuben Larson as board members.

By mid-April things were moving along rapidly, and Clarence found himself in Columbus, Ohio, chairing a meeting of sixty men interested in missionary radio. By now Clarence had edited the footage he had shot with his movie camera in Ecuador, and he showed the film to the men at the gathering.

The men were most impressed with the firsthand view the movie gave them of Ecuador.

One of the men present at the meeting, G. A. Jacobson, was exploring opportunities for using radio in Shanghai, China. As G. A. Jacobson told the group what he was doing, Clarence could see the possibilities of using radio around the world. In fact, back at the annual Missionary Alliance Conference in Quito, Clarence, Reuben Larson, Stuart and John Clark, and Paul Young had talked about those very possibilities. As they had prayed about it and read their Bibles, they felt God giving them a blueprint for how they were to proceed. And now Clarence felt that he should tell the men in Columbus, Ohio, about that blueprint.

"Why don't you open your Bibles to Acts 1:8," Clarence said and then proceeded to read the verse aloud. "'But ye shall receive power, after that the Holy Ghost is come upon you: and ye shall be witnesses unto me both in Jerusalem, and in all Judea, and in Samaria, and unto the uttermost part of the earth.'"

Clarence went on to explain how the verse held a blueprint for the ministry of Radio HCJB. "We are first to be witnesses in Jerusalem. We take this to mean that first we must broadcast locally to Quito. We must do this in Spanish, using a radio wavelength that ensures that the city's 150,000 inhabitants receive good reception. When this is done, then we are to go to Judea. This means establishing another transmitter so that we can broadcast on a medium wavelength to the rest of Ecuador and to the neighboring countries. Then third, we are to go to Samaria. This we take to mean Central and South America, where there are nearly one hundred million Spanish-speaking people. Reaching this audience is a big challenge, but it is a challenge that in due time God will help us meet. And then there are the uttermost parts of the world—the whole world. Broadcasting to the whole world may seem unattainable at this point, but as we know, with God all things are possible.

"So you see, we first start locally, and then step-by-step we move out to the rest of the world. In that respect, radio is the next missionary, for it gives us a way to reach the whole world with the gospel."

It was a bold vision, but a vision Clarence believed God would one day bring to pass. And as the men talked and prayed about the blueprint, they decided to set up a committee to collect data on just how many radio stations there were around the world and whether any of them carried Christian programs.

Meanwhile Katherine, who had stayed in Oklahoma with the children, had wonderful news. The missions secretary of the Chicago Gospel Tabernacle had called to say that someone had left a legacy to the church to be used where it was most needed. Amazingly, the secretary had decided that the money would best be used by paying off the Joneses' two-thousand-dollar debt so that they could move ahead with their plans to move to Ecuador.

"Praise God!" Clarence exclaimed. "I feel like a cork that has been weighted to a stone and suddenly set free to bob to the surface. Hold on to your hat, Kath. God is moving fast, and we are going to have to run to keep up with Him!"

Clarence was finally debt free. At the end of December, he had managed to pay back the six hundred dollars to Reuben, and now he could focus on getting together the money he would need to get himself and the family and all the necessary radio equipment to Quito.

As Clarence busily promoted and raised money for the new radio station in Quito, many Christian leaders caught the vision and encouraged and supported him. A friend from his days at Moody Bible Institute, Howard Ferrin, was now president of Providence Bible Institute in Rhode Island, and he promoted Clarence and the radio station in Ecuador everywhere he went. Dr. Walter Turnbull, leader of the Christian and Missionary Alliance, also threw his support behind Clarence and the radio station, as did Paul Rader and the Chicago Gospel Tabernacle. Gerald Winrod allowed Clarence to use his extensive mailing list to promote the new ministry. And Bob Brown, leader of the Omaha Christian Tabernacle, also promoted Clarence and the new radio station, inviting Clarence to come and speak at the church.

Clarence had a pilot fly him to Omaha. They flew in a secondhand Stinson Voyager aircraft, which Clarence hoped to buy and take to Ecuador. Clarence had not forgotten the arduous trek to Dos Ríos and how it had taken nine days to cover the same distance an aircraft could cover in an hour. The Stinson Voyager, he rationalized, would benefit not only the workers at Radio HCJB but also all missionaries in Ecuador.

When Bob Brown heard of the plan, he took Clarence aside for a talk. "Clarence, this is too much. First you are trying to sell the Christian public on radio, which many still think of as the devil's tool. In addition, you are showing a movie of Ecuador, and many people think movies are also a tool of the devil. And now you want to buy an airplane to take with you. Certainly the whole idea is a sensation, and you are getting lots of press coverage as a result, but the Christian public is just not ready for it. God has called you to do radio, and that is what you must do. Ditch the aircraft and focus where God has called you. Someone else will take up the airplane idea when the time is right. In the meantime content yourself to walk into the jungle when you must go there."

Clarence thought for several minutes about what Bob had told him and then replied, "You know, you are right. The airplane, as helpful as it would be, is too much right now. It is radio God has called me to, and that's what I need to stick to."

All the promotion and speaking that Clarence and others were doing for the new radio station soon produced results. Despite the difficult economic circumstances in the United States, money and support began to roll in for the project. Eric Williams and his wife, Ann, caught the vision for the new ministry and volunteered to help Clarence set up Radio HCJB. Eric was a radio engineer who had been sent by CBS to help produce radio programs from the Chicago Gospel Tabernacle. He had sat day after day doing his job and listening to Paul Rader preach over the radio, and it was only a matter of time before he became a Christian himself. Now Eric had found a new outlet for his talents, and Clarence gladly accepted him and his wife as members of the team.

Soon Eric was busy in his garage, building the new radio station's first transmitter. It was not the 5,000-watt affair that Clarence had been promoting. God willing, that would come later, but in the meantime Eric put together a 200-watt transmitter. In many ways it was rather puny, but it was strong enough to get the station up and running and broadcasting to Quito. Clarence and Eric used some of the money collected for the project to buy other pieces of equipment they would need to operate the new station.

Finally, in late August 1931, everything was ready, and a dedication service was held at the Chicago Gospel Tabernacle to send Clarence, Eric, and Ann off as sanctioned missionaries from the church. Since Katherine was expecting a baby in early December, she was going to stay on in Chicago until the child was born, and then she and the children would join Clarence in Quito.

Clarence had painted a backdrop scene of Ecuador for the dedication, and the new, four-foot-tall radio transmitter with the call letters HCJB painted across it was placed on stage in front of the backdrop. It was an impressive sight, and as the service progressed, Clarence silently thanked God for going before him and making the impossible possible. Finally Paul Rader called Clarence up on stage to pray for him and commit him to the work of Radio HCJB in Ecuador. When he had finished praying, Paul took off his diamond-chip cufflinks and handed them to Clarence. "These will serve as a link between you and me. God bless you, dear Clarence, if not to India, then to Ecuador," he said.

Tears began to well in Clarence's eyes as he listened to Paul's words, which meant much to him. Clarence was thankful to Paul for all he had done for him over the years. But most of all Clarence was thankful to Paul for opening his eyes to the effectiveness of radio as a tool of evangelism.

In the days following the dedication service, the radio equipment and baggage were loaded into thirty-three boxes. When they had all been packed, the boxes weighed sixty-four hundred pounds. Then it was time for the boxes to head to New York City, where they were to be loaded aboard the SS *Santa Inez* for the voyage to Ecuador. When the shipping agent in New York saw the boxes marked "World Radio Missionary Fellowship," he quipped, "Where do you get this *world* stuff? With a 200-watt transmitter, you have got to be kidding!"

Clarence was undeterred as he watched the boxes being loaded aboard the ship. God had brought them this far, and He would not desert them now. It may be only a 200-watt transmitter, but in time He would open the way for larger, more powerful transmitters capable of broadcasting to the whole continent of South America and beyond. But for now God had given them a blueprint to broadcast to Quito first, and the 200-watt transmitter was up to that task.

Once the equipment and baggage were loaded aboard, Clarence and the Williamses boarded the ship, which set sail for Ecuador the following morning. Clarence's spirit soared as they sailed out of New York Harbor and headed south. If all went well, by Christmas Clarence's dream of going south with radio would become a reality as Radio HCJB began broadcasting.

Chapter 10

On the Air at Last

Two weeks after setting out from New York, the SS *Santa Inez* arrived in Guayaquil and dropped anchor in the Guayas River. The boxes of radio equipment and baggage were loaded onto a barge and taken ashore to a customs warehouse. When Clarence, Eric, and Ann made it ashore several hours later, they cleared their baggage through customs. Then the baggage was taken across the river to the railway station, where early the next morning it was loaded onto the train for the trip to Quito.

As the narrow-gauge train climbed its way up the steep switchbacks, Clarence watched Eric and Ann press their wide-eyed faces to the window to take in the sight. Ecuador was indeed a beautiful country, and Clarence knew that when Katherine and the children finally arrived, they would find themselves at home here.

Finally the train arrived in Quito, and Clarence, Eric, and Ann clambered into a taxi. Clarence gave the driver the address of the property Reuben Larson had rented with an option to buy later, and they were off. When the taxi arrived at the address, the three of them jumped out and stood in front of Quinta Corston, surveying the scene. Clarence smiled to himself. It was hard to imagine such a tranquil spot right in the middle of a bustling city. The two-and-a-half-acre property resembled a botanical garden, with its towering eucalyptus trees, magnolias, pink bougainvillea vines, roses, and lilies. There was even an orchard in one corner, with apples and peaches ripe and ready to pick. The house looked like an English cottage, complete with dark green ivy climbing the stone walls.

As Clarence, Eric, and Ann stood surveying the property, a man emerged from the house and waved. It was Reuben. "Welcome to your new home!" he yelled.

Clarence greeted Reuben warmly and introduced him to Eric and Ann. After the introduction Reuben led them on a tour of the property. As they walked, Reuben and Clarence talked about how to transform the place into a radio station.

"The living room and sun porch in the cottage would be great for the studio and control room," Clarence said, eyeing the two-foot-thick adobe walls that would make the rooms soundproof.

"I was thinking the same thing," Reuben replied. "In fact, I have a worker ready to cut a hole through the wall and put in a glass panel to observe the announcer from the control room. Of course the acoustics aren't great, but I figured you would be able to work something out." Reuben clapped Clarence on the back.

"Just one more challenge," Clarence laughed. "What about a transmitter building? Are there any suitable outbuildings on the property?"

"Only one," Reuben replied, "and I hesitate to call it a building. The last owner built a shelter for his thoroughbred sheep. It has two mud walls and a corrugated tin roof."

"That's a start," Clarence said, his mind already swirling with ways to enclose the sheep shelter and turn it into a usable facility. "And we don't have any time to lose. I've decided we should aim to be on the air on Christmas Day. That's two and a half months away. What do you think?"

"Sounds like we'll need some miracles to make that deadline," Reuben said. "But I'm willing to do my best. We'll have to think about antennas right away."

"I have some sketches in my bag. Let's get them out and go over them," Clarence said.

And so began the first of many activity-packed days as Clarence, Reuben, and Eric prepared to put Radio HCJB on the air.

Despite having been loaded and unloaded fifteen times, sometimes roughly, onto various forms of transportation since leaving Chicago, thirty of the thirty-one boxes made it safely all the way to Quito. No one, though, could account for the missing box, which was given up as lost. When Eric explained that the missing box contained all the spare radio tubes, Clarence immediately telegraphed back to the United States for more to be sent. He knew it would take months for them to arrive, and he could only hope and pray that the radio tubes they had would not break.

The antenna presented more of a problem than anticipated. The tall, steel structure that Clarence had sketched out on paper had to yield to a more practical, improvised solution—two eighty-five-foot eucalyptus poles from the telephone company. Eric, along with a group of people he had gathered off the street, pushed the two poles into upright positions and set them in the ground two hundred feet apart. Guy wires were attached to hold the poles in place, and then a single antenna wire was strung between the poles. Two pulleys, one at the top of each pole, had been attached to hold the antenna wire before the poles were hoisted into place. But now that the poles were up, there was a problem—how to get the wire to the top of the pole and around the pulleys. The answer turned out to be Pedro, the gardener's small son. Pedro shimmied up first one pole and then the other with the end of a rope between his teeth. At the top of each pole he fed the rope around the pulley. Attached to the rope was the antenna wire. As the men on the ground tugged at the rope, the rope pulled the antenna wire into place around the pulleys, and then the wire was secured in place. Before it had been hoisted into place, Clarence and Eric had carefully measured the antenna wire several times to make sure it was the exact length to broadcast at 50.26 meters, or 5,986 kilocycles, the broadcast frequency the station had been assigned.

While Eric was busy erecting the antenna, Clarence fixed the acoustic problem in the "studio" by placing the microphone inside the two-by-four-foot packing case that the transmitter had been packed in. He lined the case with some of his mother's old velvet drapes that some of the radio parts had been packed in.

With the acoustic problem solved, Clarence, with the help of their Indian gardener, set to work adding two more walls to the sheep shelter to completely enclose it, and then the two men laid a concrete floor in the place. When the walls were finished and the floor laid, they whitewashed the adobe walls inside and out. When they were done, it was hard to tell that the structure had once been an open-ended sheep shelter. With the shed complete, Eric began moving in the transmitter and setting it up.

Clarence also had the matter of what to do with the radio receivers to think about. True to their word, the Reed brothers in Guayaquil had imported six radio receivers and sent them on up to Clarence in Quito. These six radios brought the total number of radio receivers in Ecuador to thirteen. Now Clarence and Reuben had to come up with a strategy of how best to deploy the receivers.

While the final touches to the radio station were being made, Clarence had something else on his mind. It was nearly time for Katherine to give birth, and Clarence waited anxiously for news from the United States. Finally a telegram arrived at Quinta Corston on December 15, 1931, Clarence's thirty-first birthday. It was a boy! Clarence was overjoyed. Everything had gone well with the delivery, Katherine was recovering, and Clarence could hardly wait for her and the children to arrive in Ecuador so that he could see and hold his new son. That night Clarence sat down and penned a poem to his son. Verse one read,

> Dear little fellow—newcomer, dear,
> Welcome you are, and cherished here;
> Sorry I was not there the day
> You came into our lives to stay
> Bringing us joy—
> My little boy!

The fourth verse read,

> We've called you Richard Wesley, son.
> One was my pal's name—mine is one,
> Just be like him—you'll make me glad—
> Welcome! my son, from your faraway dad.

Promise of joy,
My little boy.

By now it was only ten days until Radio HCJB was scheduled to go on the air, and Clarence, Reuben, and Eric worked at a frantic pace. As often as he could, Stuart Clark came and helped, as did John and Ruth Clark and Paul Young whenever they happened to be in Quito. Many other missionaries from various denominations in and around Quito also came to help out when they could.

On Christmas Eve everything was ready, and Clarence and Eric decided to test the system one last time. As Clarence flipped the transmitter dial, he heard a crackling noise and then saw a flash of blue light. His heart skipped a beat as he turned to Eric.

"That was the power tube," Eric wailed. "It's blown, and we don't have a spare. They were all in the box that went missing."

"God, show us what to do," Clarence prayed aloud. Then he remembered that Ecuador had one lone ham radio operator, a man who lived 120 miles away in Riobamba.

"I have to go and see if I can borrow a new one," Clarence said as he headed for the door. "I'm off to Riobamba. It's a six-hour drive in the best conditions. Pray that I make it back in time."

Clarence drove the car south over a bumpy and at times deeply rutted road, but finally he made it to Riobamba, where he inquired at a local store as to where Carlos Córdovez lived. Clarence roared up in the car to the front door of Señor Córdovez's home and rushed inside. He introduced himself and explained why he had come. Although Señor Córdovez did not have a spare tube—a blue mercury power rectifier—he did something that surprised Clarence. Using a screwdriver, he opened up the cover on his own radio transmitter. Then he reached inside and gently removed the needed power tube and handed it to Clarence. "You may borrow my tube. This should get you broadcasting," he said as he handed it over.

"Señor Córdovez, you are truly a gracious man. I thank you for the tube. I know God will bless you for your kindness," Clarence said. With that he was on his way again, headed back up the bumpy road for Quito, the precious tube wrapped in a blanket on the seat beside him.

It was Christmas morning when Clarence arrived back in Quito. Everyone breathed a deep sigh of relief when he walked through the door at Quinta Corston with the power tube in his hand. Eric quickly went to the transmitter room to install it, though he did not have time to test the tube. As far as everyone could tell, they were ready for their first broadcast, scheduled for 4:00 that afternoon.

Clarence looked at his watch. It was five minutes to four. Everyone was in his or her position. Eric was in the transmitter room, and Clarence knew that he would be frantically praying that the new power tube worked properly and they were able to transmit. Ann sat behind the console in the next room, ready to control the broadcast. Ruth sat at the organ, looking over the music, and Clarence held his trombone. Off to the side, Reuben and Stuart were going over their notes for the messages they would each deliver.

As soon as the clock struck four, Ruth cranked up the organ, and Clarence joined her on the trombone as they played the hymn "Great Is Thy Faithfulness." When they were done playing, Reuben leaned into the microphone and announced, "*Esta es la Voz de los Andes, Radiodifusora HCJB*" (This is the Voice of the Andes, Radio HCJB). Then it was time for Erma Clark and Edna Figg, a teacher from the Christian and Missionary Alliance school, to sing a duet. When they were done, John Clark stepped up to the microphone and delivered a prayer. His brother Stuart followed him to the microphone and gave a brief message in English. And then it was Reuben's turn to preach in Spanish.

Clarence felt goose bumps on his arms as he listened to Reuben for the first time ever deliver the gospel over the radio in a foreign land. Of course Clarence could not help but also wonder what was going on in the transmitter room. Was the tube working properly? Was the program really being broadcast? And was anyone listening to it? Clarence hoped so. In the end he and Reuben had decided to distribute to various government officials the six radio receivers the Reed brothers had sent them. Now he hoped not only that those officials were listening but also that they had gathered a crowd to listen along with them.

Clarence did not have to wait long to find out whether anyone had been listening. Half an hour after the broadcast ended, the hand-cranked telephone began to ring with people calling to thank the missionaries for the broadcast and wishing them well. Clarence was elated. The dream of using radio as a foreign missionary tool had finally come to pass.

After eating a Christmas feast together and celebrating their first successful broadcast, they all took their places again in the studio, control room, and transmitter room. It was time for the second broadcast of the day. This time it was a program in English. And, as after the first broadcast, when the show was over, the telephone began to ring with English-speaking listeners calling to say how much the broadcast meant to them.

Late that night an exuberant Clarence sat in his room and wrote a letter to Katherine. He hoped that she'd had a good Christmas with the three children and that she would soon be joining him in Quito. "It's a peculiar thrill to stand back of the microphone here," he wrote, "and realize that we are actually beginning the blessed work to which we have looked forward for so long."

Indeed the work was just beginning, but Clarence knew that if they were to follow the blueprint God had given them, they had much hard work ahead of them.

Chapter 11

A Growing Schedule of Programs

There's someone I want you to meet," Stuart Clark said to Clarence. "I think she's the answer to our prayers."

"What do you mean?" Clarence asked, running over in his mind some of the prayer requests he made daily for Radio HCJB.

Just then a petite woman with dark hair entered the room. Her face radiated joy.

"Señora Carmela Ochoa, I would like to introduce you to our director, Clarence Jones." The two shook hands as Stuart continued. "I met Señora Ochoa in a store yesterday. She had been lent a radio and was listening to our daily Bible program. We talked about the gospel, and as a result she has given her life to Christ."

"Why, that's wonderful," Clarence said, enthusiastically pumping Carmela's hand some more.

"And there is even more good news," Stuart added. "Señora Ochoa's first language is Spanish, but she is also fluent in Quechua. She learned it from her maid when she was a child. Now she wants to train to preach on the radio in Quechua."

Clarence paused to take it all in. Was it possible that a Spanish-speaking woman had been converted and now wanted to preach on the radio, all in a couple of days? Why not? Hadn't he and the others been praying for such a miracle?

Quechua was the language spoken by millions of South American Indians in Peru, Bolivia, Colombia, and Ecuador. A good Quechua speaker was a key that could open many doors of opportunity. Over the next several weeks, Clarence spent many hours training Carmela both in her new faith and in how to go about sharing the gospel over the radio. He was quickly astounded by the grasp she had of spiritual matters and her aptitude for radio preaching and teaching. By March 1932 Clarence felt confident enough in Carmela to launch a half-hour Bible program in Quechua. Carmela proved herself equal to the task.

Soon after launching the new program in Quechua, Clarence received a letter from Katherine. She was finally ready to make the journey to Quito with the three children. She explained that she would have come sooner, but daughters Marian and Marjorie had both had whooping cough. Clarence was overjoyed with their plans. After seven long months he was looking forward to finally being reunited with his wife and meeting his now three-month-old son. In mid-May Clarence hurriedly made his way to Guayaquil, where on May 22 he welcomed Katherine and the children to Ecuador.

It was a wonderful reunion, and the train trip back up the mountains to Quito was exciting as Clarence bounced baby Dick on his knee and watched as six-year-old Marian and four-year-old Marjorie peered happily out the window at the country that was to be their new home. Throughout the two-day trip, Clarence and Katherine caught each other up on all of their news.

Thankfully Katherine fell in love with Quinta Corston as soon as she saw the place, and the girls loved their new home as well. It was not long before the children had convinced Clarence to buy them a pet parrot and a tiny white poodle, which Marian named Rags.

With his wife and children at his side, Clarence fell into an enjoyable routine. Katherine took care of running the household and caring for the numerous guests who flowed through the house, leaving Clarence time to broaden the scope of programs offered by Radio HCJB.

When they were drawing up the proposal for the radio station back in Chicago, Clarence and the others had envisaged the station offering educational, cultural, and religious programs. They now had several daily religious programs up and running, and it was time to branch out. Clarence began *The University of the Air*, which featured broadcasts on health, hygiene, and practical agriculture. Two men, Carlos Andrade Marín, the secretary to the president, and Francisco Cruz, a university professor, worked tirelessly to promote these programs. Clarence was delighted to attract such high-caliber men to the station, even though they did not hold the same religious views.

Music had always played a big part in Clarence's life, so it was only natural that it played a prominent part in the radio broadcasts. Despite his love for playing gospel tunes and rousing John Philip Sousa marches, Clarence was conscious that the music they broadcast over the radio should reflect national tastes, and so he brought together the HCJB Ecuadorian Orchestra. It was one of the first groups in the country to write down native songs and arrange them, and Clarence liked nothing better than to get out his trombone and lead the wind section. Katherine, who had once aspired to be a concert pianist, pumped out tunes on a wheezy old organ. And when she got tired from pumping the instrument with her feet, the gardener's son Pedro would get down on his hands and knees and continue to pump it for her as she played. The girls also had a part to play. Both Marian and Marjorie had sweet voices and would sing duets or sometimes form a trio with Katherine.

It was not long before any missionary or Christian leader who came through Quito realized that he would not be leaving the city before he had sung, played an instrument, or preached on the radio. Clarence seemed to have a sixth sense for discovering who was visiting town at any particular time and for hunting him down and putting him on the radio.

News was also something that most people expected to hear on the radio, and Clarence made a modest start in this area. Each morning he read the first edition of the local newspaper and took notes on the important articles. He then wrote a summary of the articles, which he read on the air. It was a crude beginning, but many people soon came to rely on the Radio HCJB news broadcasts.

Clarence was also granted permission to broadcast the sessions of Congress when they were in progress. In this way many citizens of Ecuador heard for the first time how their government functioned.

During this time Clarence put in longer working hours than ever before. Because more and more regular programs were being broadcast, business and planning meetings were held late at night, often going on until 1:00 AM. And when he was not in the studio, Clarence was out and about in Quito, promoting the radio station and selling radio receivers. At first people were reluctant to invest their money in a receiver, but as they began to realize how helpful and informative a radio could be to their everyday lives, it was not long before there was a line of eager customers wanting to buy radio receivers.

All those who worked at the radio station were concerned about the number of poor people in the country who could not afford a radio. To help combat this situation, Clarence arranged for fifty HCJB listening posts to be set up around the country. These listening posts quickly became known as *la cajita magica que canta* (the little magic box that sings)!

Marion Krekler, an American who came to work with the radio station in Quito, also worked on the problem. In the evenings, in the dining room of his small home, Marion took out his soldering iron, and from parts he'd had shipped in from the United States, he began constructing small radio receivers. The receivers were permanently tuned to HCJB's frequency and were given to Christians with the expectation that they would make the station's programs available to their families and friends. Much to Clarence's delight, this approach worked well. Soon positive reports were flowing back from the countryside to the HCJB studios in Quito. A tailor wrote that he and sixty-five neighbors crammed into his home to listen regularly to the radio broadcasts, and a cotton worker got word to Clarence that he gathered all of the children in his village to listen to the Sunday-school broadcast each week. This was the only Bible teaching or music that the children heard, and the children were now competing to see who could learn the most Bible verses each week.

Catholic priests were also coming to the studio at Quinta Corston, asking for radio receivers. One of them told Clarence, "I want a radio that speaks softly, so no one can hear that I am listening to *la*

Voz de los Andes. All the other priests in my area have radios, and they listen too, though we do not talk to each other about it."

Of course, new listeners meant new challenges and opportunities, which Clarence and his small team rose to meet. *Sunday School of the Air* was launched to reach out to the increasing number of children listening to Radio HCJB, and Grace Larson became a popular talk-show host for young mothers. In addition, *University of the Air* branched out into broadcasting basic English lessons, and Clarence enlisted his family in a crazy program called *The Spanish Galleon.* He wrote the scripts for the show himself, with the hope that the stories would inform the Ecuadorian people of their heritage. The program featured such things as tales of pirates, with Marjorie screaming in the background and Marian dragging chains across the floor to add sound effects, and songs that Clarence made up to go along with the stories.

In the meantime, Stuart Clark opened his home for an English fellowship on Sunday afternoons. It was a formal affair, attended by the British ambassador and other dignitaries from Quito's English-speaking community. The fellowship afternoons provided a wonderful bridge between English-speaking Christians and the mainly Spanish-language radio station.

Things were moving fast, and there was never quite enough money to keep up with Clarence's latest idea. The financial situation became serious at times, and Clarence was relieved when Carlos Andrade Marin, who had left his job as the president's secretary to become the principal of a large boys' school, invited Clarence to teach English there. The arrangement suited Clarence well. Clarence taught for two hours each day and had 150 students in his classes. The students were the sons of the most influential families in the capital, and Clarence realized that it was a golden opportunity to reach them with the gospel. Since no textbooks were available for his classes, he sought permission from Carlos Andrade Marin to use the Bible as a textbook for part of his English lessons. Permission was granted, and soon many boys were seeking Clarence out for discussions on spiritual matters.

Clarence decided to accept another paid position: the director of the Quito Municipal Band. The band performed every Sunday afternoon at El Ejido Plaza in town, and its music was broadcast once a week over the radio from the HCJB studio at Quinta Corston.

Around this time, Clarence met Dr. Manuel Garrido Aldama, a converted Roman Catholic priest from Spain. After attending Bible college in Scotland, Dr. Aldama had gone to Peru to serve as a missionary. At first, he told Clarence, he had been skeptical of using radio as a tool for spreading the gospel, but he had changed his mind when he learned how people were responding to the radio broadcasts. Dr. Aldama had such a deep knowledge of Roman Catholicism and Latin culture and spoke such wonderful Spanish that Clarence invited him to host a regular broadcast on HCJB. It was an inspired decision, because Dr. Aldama's broadcast soon had a huge audience and people began writing to the studio. "We stay home from the movies to hear what Dr. Aldama has to say," they remarked.

Carmela Ochoa's program in Quechua was also increasing in popularity every day, and it, along with Dr. Aldama's program, provided a strong programming backbone to the radio station.

As could be predicted, the more hours Radio HCJB was on the air, the more widely recognized the station became. It came as no surprise to Clarence when in March 1933 HCJB was invited to be a part of the Silver Anniversary Train that would be journeying from Guayaquil to Quito to celebrate the first twenty-five years of the Guayaquil–Quito railway line. The only thing holding Clarence back from becoming involved in the celebration was the fact that Katherine was once again pregnant and might give birth while he was away. But after praying about it, Clarence decided that he should leave his wife in the capable care of Grace Larson and make the most of the opportunity presented to him.

The Silver Anniversary Exposition Train, as it was officially called, would make its journey in June, and when Clarence arrived in Guayaquil to join the train, he was surprised. The narrow-gauge steam engine had been cleaned and repainted black and gold, the boxcars that made up the train had been repainted in bright colors, and a large banner on the side declared that it was indeed the Silver Anniversary Exposition Train. The boxcars contained displays of various aspects of Ecuadorian culture, science, and industry. The Radio HCJB boxcar, the first carriage in the train, was hooked onto the back of the engine.

The HCJB boxcar had been decked out with cots for Clarence and Stuart Clark to sleep on; a table stacked with Spanish Bibles, New Testaments, and tracts; a portable organ, a phonograph, a microphone, Clarence's trombone, and a small radio transmitter. On top of the boxcar was mounted a 50-watt loudspeaker.

Clarence was filled with anticipation as the train pulled away from the station in Guayaquil. For the first leg of the journey, he rode on the roof of the boxcar, filming the journey with his movie camera. The train rolled along across the flatland outside of Guayaquil and then made its way through a canyon, where the railway tracks ran alongside the surging Chan-Chan River. Finally it came to a small, rural enclave, the first stop on the journey. When the train pulled to a halt in the town, Clarence slipped inside the boxcar. Moments later the Ecuadorian national anthem began to blare from the loudspeaker atop the boxcar. Clarence watched in amusement as the startled residents of the town flocked to the boxcar, their jaws slack with wonder. In the twenty-five years the train had been passing through their town, the people had never encountered a "singing boxcar." As the last notes of the national anthem faded away, Stuart pulled open the door to the boxcar to reveal Clarence standing in front of the microphone, his trombone at the ready. Clarence then began to play a rousing march, to which the people of the town cheered and clapped in delight, most of them never having heard a trombone before.

When Clarence was done playing, the Minister of Agriculture and Commerce stepped up to the microphone. "We are here to do honor to the intrepid vision and courage that built this railroad...." But as he spoke, the gathered crowd cut him off with the chant, "Music, we want more music."

Finally the obviously frustrated minister stepped aside and handed the microphone back to Clarence. This time Clarence sat and played the portable organ and sang a number of Ecuadorian tunes, encouraging those in the crowd to sing along with him. After several minutes of singing, Clarence delivered a short message telling the people about how Jesus Christ could change their lives. When he was done, Clarence encouraged the people to visit the displays in the various boxcars of the train, promising them that if they did this he would play more music for them later.

The same scene greeted Clarence and Stuart in all the towns they stopped at along the way, and by the time they made it back to Quito, Clarence was exuberant. Not only had people learned about Radio HCJB as a result of the trip, but also Clarence and Stuart had been able to personally share their faith with many hundreds of Ecuadorians.

For Clarence the future was filled with promise as he made his way back to Quinta Corston. Clarence had no way of knowing that things were about to take a turn for the worse.

Chapter 12

Crisis and Growth

The letters Clarence received from the United States told of how things were as tight there financially as they were in Quito. As the economic depression deepened, many people who had promised to financially support the new radio mission were struggling to put food on the table for their families. The Chicago Gospel Tabernacle had started a food bank that had been inundated with middle-class families who needed help to make ends meet and survive. As a result of the worsening economic situation, during 1932 less than one thousand dollars had been sent from Christians in the United States to help support the Jones and Williams families as well as the work of HCJB.

Clarence and Katherine did what they could to make the donated money go as far as possible.

They padded the soles of the girls' shoes with layers of cardboard, and when the new baby was born—another girl, whom they named Nancy—Katherine made most of her clothes. They also planted a huge garden at Quinta Corston, and Katherine busied herself canning hundreds of jars of produce. Sometimes it was all the family had to eat.

By mid-1933 the situation had become serious. Clarence was now getting reports that banks were failing in the United States and that people who had once been well-off were selling their homes and moving in with relatives to make ends meet. Then came even worse news. The bank that held the Chicago Gospel Tabernacle's savings failed, and the church lost its money. Paul Rader wrote to Clarence, explaining the dire situation the church was in and apologizing for the fact that no more support money would be coming from them for the Jones family and the radio ministry.

Clarence was stunned when he read Paul's letter. There was no way that his two part-time jobs could keep them all afloat financially. He wondered what had gone wrong. Had HCJB all been a mistake? Had God really led him to Quito, or had it all been his own idea? For the first time since arriving in Ecuador, Clarence began to have severe doubts about whether he was in the right place. The turmoil he felt was made all the greater when an electric bill for $6.15 arrived in the mail. Clarence had no money to pay the bill, and without electricity there could be no radio station. It was one of the worst times in

Clarence's life as he stared at the bill on the table. Would the whole ministry go under from owing less than seven dollars? It seemed likely.

Not knowing what else to do, Clarence took the bill and a kitchen chair down to the toolshed at the back of the Quinta Corston property. He sat down and poured out his heart in prayer. As he prayed, he called to mind once again Jeremiah 33:3: "Call unto me, and I will answer thee." *Yes,* Clarence thought, *God will answer me—not my supporters, who are themselves in dire financial straits, not the church or Paul Rader, but God will answer me.* Then it was as if a voice inside Clarence said, "Yes, I will answer. I'll show you great and mighty things—bigger than you've ever dreamed of!" Hope welled up in Clarence's heart at this, and by the time he left the toolshed, he was confident that God was going to do "something new," that a miracle was just around the corner.

The following day Stuart paid Clarence a visit. "Something's been bothering you for the past few days," he noted.

"Yes, it has," Clarence began and proceeded to lay out the woeful condition of his family's and the radio station's finances.

Stuart listened quietly to Clarence and then offered to advance money to cover the bill and provide some financial relief for the family. "You also need to go and talk to the bank manager and see what arrangements you can make with him for the future."

Clarence thanked Stuart for his generosity and advice, and two days later he went to see the local bank manager. After some discussion, he arranged a mortgage with the bank on HCJB's transmitter that would allow the station to pay its next round of bills. It was not quite the miracle Clarence had been hoping for, but as he noted, "Climbing is not always going forward; sometimes you go sideways, looking for a better way to climb the mountain."

One of those better ways to climb the mountain was to produce a flyer to send to supporters, promoting the radio station and listing the station's specific financial needs. For the flyer Clarence composed a poem that he titled "The Call of the Andes."

Where blue skies are swelling
The Andes are telling
Of dark shadows dwelling—
So long;
Where darkness is falling
Sad hearts there are calling
With sorrows enthralling
Too long.
But now o'er the Andes there comes beaming
The Gospel of Life, brightly gleaming,
And still, where sin is betraying
And burdens are weighed
The Andes are saying—
"How long?"

In the flyer Clarence laid out the situation facing Radio HCJB:

- We have had to mortgage our transmitter, the heart of our work.
- We need $5,000 to purchase this property.
- We believe that God has inspired and will prosper HCJB—four letters that mean South America's greatest chance to hear the gospel in this generation.

Clarence also included in the flyer the testimonies of several people whose lives had been changed and blessed through "hearing the gospel in this new way."

Once the flyer was printed, Clarence sent it out to all of HCJB's supporters. Despite the difficult economic times, money began to flow in to HCJB for the first time ever. Soon they had enough money not only to pay off the mortgaged transmitter but also to buy the Quinta Corston property. Buying the property had just one hitch to it, however. Ecuadorian law stated that any land bought in Ecuador by foreigners reverted back to the government after five years. There was no way a radio station could thrive if it had to buy back its own property every few years.

Clarence took the problem to Ecuador's Congress. After thinking about the situation for several days, the leader of the congress finally stood up and declared, "Gentlemen, I am standing before a microphone of HCJB. Through the courtesy of HCJB, all the citizens of Ecuador know what this government is doing. I would like to propose that HCJB be exempt from the ruling on foreign-owned property."

A vote was soon taken, and every member of the congress voted in favor of the exemption. Now Clarence could buy Quinta Corston, and the property would remain in HCJB ownership. This was a tremendous relief to Clarence, not only because it meant that the station could stabilize its situation but also because the vote represented a significant endorsement of HCJB by the government.

With the matter taken care of, Clarence arranged for a well-earned vacation for his family. The Joneses climbed aboard the train with three weeks' worth of supplies for the trip to Guayaquil. From Guayaquil they made their way to the Isle of Puna at the mouth of the Guayas River, where John Reed let them stay at his vacation retreat. The place was basically a fisherman's hut made of split bamboo. It had a thatched roof and sat on stilts right on the beach. The setting was idyllic. At high tide the water came right under the place, and at low tide Clarence and the children would play softball on the beach. They would also swim in the surf and take long walks along the white-sand beach, exploring the many calm, crystal-clear coves around the island. Clarence loved to sit on the beach and watch the sun set across the sparkling Pacific Ocean, and at night the three older children slept under the stars on the porch, where sometimes Clarence joined them.

After three wonderful weeks of relaxing in the warm, tropical sun, the Jones family reluctantly made its way back to Quito. Clarence arrived rejuvenated and with his mind full of new ideas for radio programs and ways to promote HCJB.

At the radio station Clarence relied heavily on Reuben and Grace Larson for help with the Spanish programming. Not long after Clarence's return from vacation, however, tragedy struck the Larsons. Grace gave birth to a baby, but the child did not live long. After the ordeal, Grace went to stay at Quinta Corston, where Katherine could help her recover from the loss. Despite Katherine's best efforts, Grace's mental and physical health did not greatly improve. By mid-1934 Reuben was so worried about his wife that he decided to take her back to the United States to get more medical attention. The decision was a blow to Clarence. Not only did it add to his workload at the radio station, but also Clarence took over many of Reuben's missionary duties for the Christian and Missionary Alliance.

In fact, it was taking care of one of these duties that nearly cost Clarence his life. Clarence was keeping an eye on things in Dos Ríos and was on his way back to Quito after delivering supplies when disaster struck. The guides had risen early, around 4:00 AM, and had set off in the dark along the narrow horse trail carved from the mountainside. Clarence was bringing up the rear of the group as they made their way along. It had rained during the night, and the trail was slippery. Clarence's horse suddenly stumbled on the treacherous trail and slid right over the edge, taking Clarence with it.

Clarence barely had time to take in what had happened. One moment he was riding along the trail on the back of his horse, and suddenly the next moment he and his horse were falling toward the floor of the canyon over one thousand feet below. Clarence had not even been able to open his mouth and utter a desperate prayer or a scream to alert the others to his fate, when the horse's bridle caught on a branch of a tree, jerking the animal. The jerk was enough to change the trajectory of their fall, and horse and rider collapsed onto a small ledge. The horse was splayed across Clarence's left leg, pinning Clarence in place. Immediately he called out to the guides, who had been riding ahead of him, but there was no response. Clarence began to fret that this was the end. He was trapped on a narrow ledge in the dark with his horse lying on top of him, and no one knew where he was. One wrong move by him or the horse could quickly send them both off the ledge and careening again toward the canyon bottom. The minutes passed slowly as Clarence silently prayed and wondered what to do while trying to keep the shocked horse calm.

Dawn began to break across the Andes, affording Clarence his first view of the situation. It was more precarious than he had imagined. The ledge was so small that he was amazed they had actually landed on it and stopped falling. The early dawn light also illuminated the only means of escape, back up the steep rock face to the trail above. But before he could try that, he had to get the horse off him without falling off the ledge himself. Clarence was just about to try when he heard someone calling. "Are you there? Can we help you?"

"Yes. Down here! Come and help get this horse off me," he yelled back, trying not to spook the horse.

Moments later the faces of his guides appeared over the edge of the trail above. Clarence had never been more delighted to see them than he was at that moment. The guides quickly sized up the situation, lowered a rope, and carefully climbed down to the ledge. Clarence was not quite sure how the guides managed to do it, but somehow, with one of them taking the horse by the head and the other holding it by the tail, they skillfully encouraged the animal back up onto the trail a hundred feet above. Then they helped Clarence back up to the trail, where he discovered that his left leg was stiff and bruised from the horse being on it, although no bones were broken. The men walked on a few yards to where the trail was a little wider and built a fire and boiled some water for coffee. As Clarence sipped the steaming drink, the guides told him that as dawn broke they realized he was no longer with the group. So they had turned around and come back to look for him, fearing the worst—that he had slipped off the trail and fallen all the way to the canyon floor below and been killed. They were relieved when they found him alive. Clarence heartily agreed with them!

When he had drained his cup of coffee, Clarence mounted his horse, and the group set out for Quito again. As he rode, Clarence's mind buzzed with ways to work the story of the fall into a radio sermon.

One good thing that resulted from Reuben and Grace Larson's return to the United States was the setting up of a home advisory council for the World Radio Missionary Fellowship. This group of twenty-five Christian leaders, comprising pastors, missionaries, educators, and businessmen, agreed to support the work of the World Radio Missionary Fellowship in whatever way they could—from helping to raise money for the work in Ecuador to praying for it, promoting it, and encouraging the staff in their work. It was tremendously encouraging to Clarence to know that a group of people was out there that was equally as committed as he was to seeing the ministry of Radio HCJB grow and flourish and reach out to more and more people with the gospel.

December 1935 marked HCJB's fourth anniversary. The time had flown by so fast that it was hard for Clarence to realize that four years had passed since they had gathered on Christmas Day for their first broadcast. How the ministry had grown in the intervening years! A wide range of programs was now offered each day over the airwaves, and the programs were being listened to by people throughout Ecuador. According to the letters they received, people in the neighboring countries of Peru and Colombia were also tuning in to listen to the programs. But it was still the same 200-watt transmitter that Eric Williams had built back in Chicago that was broadcasting the programs, reaching farther afield than Clarence could have imagined. The transmitter had worked flawlessly for almost the full four years, keeping the radio station on the air with uninterrupted transmission, so much so that the transmitter had been nicknamed "Old Faithful." But of late, Old Faithful had begun to suffer a number of breakdowns and tube burnouts. And so, as the fourth anniversary rolled around, Clarence knew that it was time to start thinking about a new, more modern transmitter.

All those involved with the radio station agreed that it was time for a new transmitter. Now the question became, how powerful should the transmitter be, and on what frequency should it broadcast?

For guidance in answering these two questions, Clarence turned to the blueprint based on Acts 1:8 that he, Stuart and John Clark, Reuben Larson, and Paul Young had developed five years before. According to the blueprint they were already broadcasting to Jerusalem (Quito) and Judea (Ecuador). Now it was time to concentrate on broadcasting to Samaria—the rest of South and Central America. With this goal in mind they settled on a broadcast frequency of thirty-six meters and agreed that the new transmitter should have at least one kilowatt of power.

Of course, such a powerful transmitter would not be cheap, and a new fundraising campaign would have to be launched to raise the needed money to buy it. But Clarence was confident that before long Radio HCJB would be broadcasting to an even wider audience with a new, powerful transmitter.

While plans were being made for the new transmitter, HCJB received a gift of money earmarked for the evangelization of Ecuador. As Clarence pondered where best to spend the money, an idea came to him. He thought back to his time on the Silver Anniversary Exposition Train in 1933. The HCJB boxcar on this train had been a huge success. People had flocked to the "singing boxcar" to listen to the music and hear the gospel being preached. *Why not do the same thing again?* Clarence wondered. Only this time, rather than using a boxcar, he would use a truck, which could travel the length and breadth of Ecuador, sharing the gospel in small towns and villages. And so the ministry of Radio Rodante (rolling radio) was born.

An International truck was purchased for the purpose. Onto the back of it was built a custom-designed canopy with large doors at the back that could swing wide open. The truck was fitted inside with cabinets and compartments that held tracts and Bibles, cooking utensils, blankets and sleeping bags, and a movie projector and reels of film. A generator sat in one corner behind the cab, and a transmitter that powered the large, bell-shaped loudspeakers that were attached to the roof sat in the opposite corner.

Clarence was very impressed when he viewed the finished sound bus, as the vehicle was referred to. He wished he were going along on it, but he had so much to do that this time he stayed at the radio station in Quito.

The Radio Rodante truck set out, and soon Clarence was hearing wonderful reports about its ministry. When the truck drove into a small community, it headed for the square at the center of town, where it parked and set up its loudspeakers. As soon as the speakers were up, they began to blare the Ecuadorian national anthem. As had happened with the boxcar, a crowd soon gathered around the truck as curious residents of the town came to see what was going on. Also, as with the boxcar, when a large enough crowd had gathered and the national anthem died away, those manning the truck got up behind the microphone at the back of the truck. They led the group in singing, shared the gospel, handed out tracts, and sold Spanish Bibles and New Testaments.

The response to Radio Rodante was so great that soon Clarence was thinking about adding two more sound trucks to the ministry.

As Clarence looked at the various facets of the ministry of Radio HCJB, he had to admit that from that day in mid-1933 when in desperation he had gone to the toolshed to pray, God had indeed done a "new thing" with the ministry. Back then he had had doubts as to whether the station could stay on the air because of an overdue power bill totaling $6.15. Now they owned Quinta Corston, plans were under way for a new transmitter, and people all over Ecuador were hearing the gospel either over the radio or through the ministry of Radio Rodante. Clarence was excited as he contemplated what the future held for him and Radio HCJB.

Chapter 13

A Piece of Junk

The thousand-watt (one-kilowatt) transmitter was installed at the radio station in early 1937, creating more work than ever for Clarence. The new transmitter was designed and built by Victoriano Salvador, HCJB's first full-time Ecuadorian radio engineer employee. When the installation was complete, Radio HCJB was able to reach an astounding ninety million listeners throughout South and Central America with its broadcasts. This led to new radio programs being produced and broadcast, and soon many more letters were flowing into Quinta Corston from listeners, keeping an already busy staff busier than ever answering them.

At the same time that the new transmitter was installed, Clarence bought himself a ham radio set so that he could monitor reception in various countries. Soon he was talking on the ham radio to people all over the world, and his vision for HCJB began to expand beyond South and Central America. "What would it take to broadcast around the world from Quito?" he asked himself.

In July 1937 everyone at HCJB was relieved when Reuben and Grace Larson returned to Quito. And they were all even more delighted when the Christian and Missionary Alliance recognized the important work that Radio HCJB was doing and "loaned" the Larsons to the radio station on a full-time basis. With Reuben now working as co-leader of the ministry, Clarence began to think about taking his own family home to the United States on furlough, though not just yet but sometime in the not too distant future. He still had too much work to do as they ramped up the schedule of programs being broadcast to a wider audience.

In the midst of increasing the number of programs offered, Clarence received a letter from a well-known radio evangelist in the United States named Charles Fuller. In the letter Mr. Fuller explained that he wanted to reach a wider audience with his *Old-Fashioned Revival Hour* radio show. To achieve this end, he was willing to send down to Ecuador seventeen-inch phonograph disc recordings of the shows and pay for them to be broadcast on HCJB.

Clarence was very excited by the letter. Using recorded discs meant that a program did not have to be broadcast live! All the musicians and speakers involved in the program would not have to be assembled in the studio at Quinta Corston. Instead the disc could be broadcast simply by placing it on a turntable. Clarence wrote back to Mr. Fuller immediately, accepting the offer and suggesting that HCJB and Mr. Fuller split the cost of broadcasting the program.

Later that year Clarence received more exciting news. A used 5,000-watt (5-kilowatt) transmitter was available for sale in Chicago for ten thousand dollars. Clarence immediately got in touch with the board of advisers for the radio station, explaining that such a transmitter would allow them to reach a much larger audience around the world with their radio signal. The response of the board of advisers was encouraging. "If this transmitter looks good and you can find the money, go ahead and buy it," they wrote back.

Now Clarence had a reason to return to the United States. In early 1938 the Jones family packed up and headed for Guayaquil. Clarence had booked passage back to the United States on a cargo vessel that had several passenger cabins aboard. When he booked the passage, Clarence had not realized that it was the vessel's maiden voyage. As a result, everything possible was done to make the twelve passengers traveling aboard extra comfortable for the journey.

This time the ship was not headed for New York City through the Panama Canal but was headed for

San Pedro, California. When the family reached San Pedro, waiting for them on the dock was Katherine's father. They all enjoyed a tearful reunion. During the six years she had been in Quito, Katherine had convinced herself that she would never see her father again. And now here they were, all standing together on the dock in San Pedro.

Following their reunion the family went and ate a hearty lunch, and then Adam Welty took Clarence to a used-car lot and arranged for him to buy a 1935 Ford. "We need something to get *seven* of us all around the country," he told his son-in-law. Clarence was surprised and delighted by the comment. His father-in-law was planning to itinerate around the country with them.

The first stop Clarence made after arriving back in the United States was a visit to Charles Fuller in Pasadena, California. The two men talked late into the night about upcoming *Old-Fashioned Revival Hour* shows and the impact past shows were having in South America.

From Southern California they all set out to travel around the country. They had little money to spare, certainly not enough to stay in hotels along the way. However, Mr. Welty came up with a plan to take care of their accommodations. Just before dark each evening he would have Clarence drive around as he looked at names on mailboxes. When Mr. Welty saw a German name that he recognized, he would ask the people who lived in the house if they were German Mennonites. Most of the time they were, and they had heard of Adam Welty and his mission in Lima, Ohio, since the Mennonites supported the mission. Once the connection was established, everyone was welcomed into the home, given a good German dinner, and put to bed on mats on the living room floor. Often one host would arrange a place for the Jones family to stay the next night.

Everywhere that Clarence went, he talked about HCJB—what they were doing and how much farther they could reach with their radio signal if they had a stronger transmitter. All across the United States he met with others involved in broadcasting Christian programs over the radio. As Clarence soon discovered, his time working at the Chicago Gospel Tabernacle was now providing him many wonderful contacts along the way.

Even though he prayed hard and gave all his effort to itinerating, by the end of 1938 Clarence had raised only one-third of the money needed to buy the 5-kilowatt transmitter. It was hard for him not to get discouraged as they headed on to Lima, Ohio, to spend their last two weeks in the United States with Katherine's family.

When they arrived in Lima, a telegram was waiting for Clarence. It came from a well-known Christian businessman named R. G. LeTourneau. Excitement welled in Clarence as he read the telegram: "If you want to see me before sailing, come!"

Clarence suddenly felt a surge of hope. R. G. LeTourneau was a prominent Christian businessman involved in inventing, building, and marketing large earthmoving equipment. He had been very successful in this and now gave 90 percent of his income to Christian work, much of it to the Christian and Missionary Alliance and the Christian Business Men's Committee.

Clarence had no idea how LeTourneau had heard of his plight, but he chartered a small airplane the next day and flew to Peoria, Illinois. His father-in-law went with him, and the two men prayed much of the way there.

When Clarence and his father-in-law arrived in Peoria, LeTourneau welcomed them warmly. "Sit down and make yourselves at home," he said. "I have heard a lot about the work of HCJB. Tell me what you are up to now and what you plan to do next."

Clarence launched into a summary of the work of Radio HCJB, including their ability to reach over ninety million people with the gospel. "But my vision is bigger than that," he concluded. "With a 5,000-watt transmitter we could send a signal around the world!"

"Interesting," LeTourneau replied. "What I would really like to sponsor is someone who would build a radio station in the Philippines to reach into Asia. If you agree to do that, I'll underwrite the entire cost of the project."

For once in his life, Clarence did not know what to say. Here was a man willing to hand him a radio station on a platter, only it was in the wrong area of the world for Clarence. Of course, Clarence had a plan to reach around the world with a network of radio stations, but a small voice in his head warned him that it was not yet the time to branch out. Clarence could not ignore this warning, which he was sure came from God, even if it meant giving up the backing of an influential and wealthy patron like R. G. LeTourneau.

The men talked on for a little longer, and then Clarence stood up. "I'm sorry, Mr. LeTourneau, but my call is to South America. As far as I can see, we still have a long way to go on that project. You will have to find someone else to start a radio station in the Philippines."

"I might do that," LeTourneau responded, "but in the meantime I would like to do what I can to help you. How much more money do you need?"

"I have raised three thousand dollars, and we need ten thousand, so we still need seven thousand dollars," Clarence said.

LeTourneau pulled a checkbook from his desk drawer and quickly wrote a check. "Keep in touch, Clarence," he said as he handed it over. "I expect to hear of good things happening in South America."

Clarence glanced at the check. It was for the full seven thousand dollars! Now he did not have to return to Quito empty-handed. He could buy the 5-kilowatt transmitter right away.

Instead of flying back to Lima, Clarence ordered the chartered airplane to fly to Chicago, where he met with the man selling the radio transmitter. Papers were hastily drawn up to sign for the sale, but as Clarence lifted his pen to sign the papers, he heard the words "don't do it" in his head. This was the last thing he had expected to hear, but he instantly recognized the words as a warning from God not to go ahead with the purchase. Instead of signing the papers, Clarence put down the pen and turned to the seller. "I'm sorry to have gone this far with the deal, but I'm afraid I can't go any further. I just don't feel free to go ahead with this purchase."

As Clarence shook the man's hand and walked out of his office, he wondered what had just happened. He had come to the United States to buy the transmitter for ten thousand dollars, he had a check for that amount in his pocket, but somehow at the last minute he felt it was the wrong thing to do. He could not explain it to himself, much less to his father-in-law or to Katherine.

A week later the Jones family was in Boston preparing to return to Ecuador. While in Boston Clarence received a phone call from John Meredith, a member of the advisory board. "Did you end up buying that transmitter?" John asked.

"No," Clarence replied. "I have all the money, but I just couldn't sign the sale documents."

"Great!" John's voice rang on the other end of the line. "It's a heap of junk!"

"How do you know that?" Clarence asked.

"My nephew Clarence Moore and another amateur radio operator took a look at it, and I've just gotten off the phone with Clarence. He told me the transmitter is obsolete. There's no way to update it. It's bound for the scrap heap."

"Really?" Clarence said as he put the pieces together in his head. No wonder he had not felt free to sign the papers for the sale!

"Yes, these boys are sharp. I think you should meet them," John replied.

"I'd like that," Clarence said. "Is there any way they could come to Boston before I leave?"

"I'll do my best to get them there. I have a feeling they're part of God's plan in this whole thing," John said.

After the phone call Clarence told Katherine and her father what he had just been told.

"Thank goodness we didn't return to Quito with a pile of junk!" Katherine exclaimed. "And who knows what God will do now."

Clarence certainly did not know what God would do next as he sat waiting the following evening for the two young men to arrive. It was New Year's Eve, and somehow Clarence Moore and Bill Hamilton had made it to Boston in less than a day to meet with Clarence. As he waited for them to arrive, Clarence sat in a hotel coffee shop reading the newspaper. So much of the international news concerned Germany. With each passing day, the German leader Adolf Hitler and his Nazi party seemed to be getting more aggressive with the rest of Europe. Some commentators were saying that it could only lead to war if something was not done to try to defuse the situation.

Finally Clarence and Bill arrived at the coffee shop, introduced themselves, and shook hands with Clarence. Not wanting to waste anyone's time,

Clarence got right to the point. "For the past year I've been trying to raise money to buy that 5,000-watt transmitter you men looked over. God has provided the money, but I didn't feel I should go ahead with the purchase. Now you tell me it would have been foolish to go ahead. But as far as I know, it's the only piece of equipment like it on the market today. So what do you suggest we do next?"

Neither Clarence Moore nor Bill spoke, and in the ensuing silence, an idea came to Clarence Jones like a bolt of lightning. "Could the two of you build us a new 5,000-watt transmitter for ten thousand dollars?" he asked.

Bill shook his head. "Impossible," he said.

But as the two young men discussed the idea, a hopeful grin began to creep across each of their faces.

"I think we just might be able do it," Clarence Moore finally announced. "Of course, lots of details would have to be worked out."

Clarence Jones reached out and patted them both on the back. "With God's help, I know you can," he said.

It was amazing how quickly the details came together. Clarence Moore, who was a high school teacher and Mennonite pastor, took a leave of absence from both jobs to oversee the mammoth project. And when Clarence Jones appraised R. G. LeTourneau of the situation, LeTourneau welcomed the change of plans and offered a corner of his manufacturing plant in Peoria as a workshop in which to build the new transmitter.

By the time Clarence boarded the ship early in the new year for the trip back to Ecuador, he was confident that Clarence Moore and Bill Hamilton would deliver a new 5,000-watt transmitter to him in Quito in twelve to eighteen months' time. He looked forward to progress reports from Peoria.

Chapter 14

Reaching the World

The news from Clarence Moore was even better than had been anticipated. Clarence had apparently been able to work out a way to double the wattage power of the transmitter for very little extra money. He had explained how to do it to R. G. LeTourneau, who in turn had provided the additional money needed to double the wattage.

Clarence Jones was delighted as he read the news in a letter from Clarence Moore. He had gone back to the United States on furlough, hoping to purchase a used 5,000-watt transmitter, and instead they would be getting a brand-new 10,000-watt (10-kilowatt) transmitter. Clarence could hardly wait for the new transmitter to arrive in Quito. But before it arrived, much work and planning had to be done.

Several big changes had taken place in Ecuador in the year Clarence had been away in the United States. The biggest change was that Shell Oil, a Dutch/British-owned company, had been granted permission to explore for oil in the Oriente. Until now, few foreigners had lived in the eastern jungles of Ecuador. The Oriente had no roads, airstrips, or sturdy bridges over its many rivers, making it a difficult place to get in and out of, as Clarence had learned firsthand. To explore for oil in the region, the Shell Oil Company had begun building a road from the town of Baños down the Andes to the place it intended to use as its base of operation in the Oriente, a place it had named Shell Mera. There, on a stretch of boggy, flat land between the Pastaza and Motolo Rivers, the company was planning to build a mile-long airstrip so that it could fly equipment and personnel into the region.

The efforts of the Shell Oil Company meant that for the first time in history, the Oriente was opening up to the outside world. Clarence was quick to realize that the opening up of the Oriente also meant opening up the region to radio. Radio receivers could be delivered to the many isolated villages throughout the area so that the Indians who lived there could hear Christian radio. Of course, this was a goal that Clarence knew would take a lot of planning before it could be carried out.

Another change had also taken place. Clarence had helped write the communication and radio laws that were now in force in Ecuador. As a result, he knew that a transmitter as powerful as the 10-kilowatt one being built by Clarence Moore could not be situated within the city limits. Radio HCJB would have to find a new home outside the city limits.

Clarence and Stuart Clark looked for a new site for the radio station and found a suitable property, a cabbage patch on the north side of Quito, outside the city limits. Since the property was larger than HCJB needed, Stuart negotiated with the Christian and Missionary Alliance to buy half of the land on which to build a new school.

Once the purchase of the property was complete, building began straightaway. First a transmitter house was constructed, and then a new home was built for the Jones family that contained ample room for missionary guests. Eager to replicate the beautiful gardens at Quinta Corston, Clarence planted avenues of stately palm trees, and he put calla lilies, roses, and geraniums in flower beds around the new house.

The building at the new site was completed by the time Clarence Moore arrived in Quito with the transmitter in September 1939. That same month news arrived that Germany had invaded Poland and that, in response, Britain and France had declared war on Germany.

The new transmitter was moved into the newly built transmitter room, and a one-hundred-foot antenna tower made from slender eucalyptus poles lashed together was erected. A rotary-beam antenna was fastened to the top of the tower. Once the antenna was up and the transmitter installed, it was time to test the new equipment.

Late one evening the phone rang in the Joneses' house at Quinta Corston (they had not yet moved into their new home), and Clarence picked it up. "Hello," he said.

"Get over here with your camera. We've got balls of fire, and music on the mountain!" Clarence Moore exclaimed from the other end of the telephone line.

Clarence headed over to the new site as quickly as he could, unsure of what Clarence Moore had meant when he said, "We've got balls of fire." But as he approached the property, the meaning quickly became clear. Four-foot-long streaks of lightning were arcing off the antenna ends, lighting up the night sky.

Clarence ran over to a bewildered-looking Clarence Moore, who stood staring up at the top of the arcing antenna. "What's the problem?" he asked.

Clarence Moore scratched his head, and still looking at the antenna, he said, "I don't know, really. No one has ever encountered this before. But of course no one has ever tried to put up a radio antenna at ninety-three-hundred feet above sea level either. But if this keeps up, the heat will eventually melt the ends off the antenna terminals."

Over the next several days, Clarence Moore finally worked out what was causing the antenna to arc. He explained to Clarence that the problem was caused by high voltage in the rarefied atmosphere at this altitude. "There has to be a way to stop it. I'm just not sure what it is," he told Clarence with a frown. "I need to get away and think about the problem for a few days."

And that is what Clarence Moore did. He packed up his technical manuals and headed to the coast. Several days later he arrived back in Quito, the puzzling frown gone from his face. "I have the solution to our problem," he told Clarence, pulling four copper toilet bowl floats from his bag. "These should do the trick."

Clarence Jones looked puzzled, and Clarence Moore explained. "I'll put one of these floats on each of the antenna terminals, basically eliminating the antenna ends where the arcing is coming from." Sure enough, the copper toilet bowl floats fixed the problem.

While he had been at the coast mulling over a solution to the arcing problem, Clarence Moore had also come up with an idea for how to improve the overall performance of the antenna. Clarence Jones watched as Clarence Moore built a square of continuous wire with a reflector behind it. When the device was all put together on a circular pad at the top of the antenna tower, it resembled a cube, which Clarence Moore called a "cubical quad" antenna. Clarence Jones was very pleased with the improved performance of the cubical quad. And since the device was made of continuous wire, it had no ends to arc in the atmosphere.

Everyone worked feverishly to get the new transmitter and antenna up and running, and when everything was finally ready, a dedication service for the new transmitter was organized. The dedication service was held on Easter Sunday, March 24, 1940. Ecuadorian President Andres Cordova attended the service, arriving with a full military escort. The American ambassador to Ecuador also attended. During the service, the president gave a speech.

"I am thankful to the Voice of the Andes that the opportunity has been given me to put into operation its machinery, closing the electric switch that gives it life. And upon declaring this new station officially inaugurated, I repeat my felicitations to its directors and give my best wishes that this enterprise, so highly respected in this country, shall continue to reap its abundant and well-earned rewards."

Then, with great pomp and ceremony, President Cordova threw the switch, and the new 10,000-watt transmitter was officially on the air.

Clarence felt tears welling in his eyes as he held Katherine's hand and watched the ceremony. He thought back to just nine years before when, on Christmas Day, HCJB went on the air for the first time with a 200-watt transmitter. Now here they were inaugurating a transmitter that was fifty times more powerful. Clarence could hardly wait to see how far around the world the signal from the new transmitter would beam.

Now that HCJB could broadcast to the world, Clarence and his team at the radio station worked hard to produce programs in a variety of languages.

Reuben could speak Swedish and started a broadcast in that language. He was soon joined at the microphone by Ellen Campaña, a Swedish woman married to a high official in the Ecuadorian government.

Peter Deyneka, Clarence's old friend from the Chicago Gospel Tabernacle who had started an organization called the Slavic Gospel Association, sent down programs to be broadcast in Russian. Many missionaries who had been forced by hostile governments out of the countries where they were serving also began arriving in Quito, ready and able to present programs and Bible readings in a variety of languages. Soon HCJB was broadcasting in eighteen languages, including German, Portuguese, Japanese, French, Yiddish, Italian, Dutch, and Czech. Clarence was happy. Finally the ministry had grown into its name—the World Radio Missionary Fellowship.

It was not long before letters began to pour in to HCJB headquarters in Quito. As Clarence saw where the letters were coming from, he was amazed at how far afield listeners were able to pick up the signal of Radio HCJB. Letters and prayer requests came from Japan, New Zealand, India, Germany, and Russia. The letters meant even more work for the staff at the radio station, since Clarence insisted that every inquiry be referred to a local missionary or pastor.

Clarence read many of the letters himself. One came from Belize in Central America:

> I am a Mayan Indian. For several years I have tuned in HCJB. I accepted Jesus as my personal Savior; my wife and two daughters also

> became believers. Our lives have changed; we now make Scripture reading our daily habit. Your programs open our vision to more spiritual living and awake my soul to help others come to Christ.

Another arrived from New Delhi, India:

> By chance I came across your station on my radio. Is it really true that by believing in Christ we can achieve salvation? I am a seventeen-year-old college student, and I have so many questions about God.

One came from Connecticut in the United States:

> I turned my shortwave radio to HCJB, and my roommate told me to turn that junk off. But I insisted that we listen. The next evening when I walked in, he already had HCJB tuned in. A week later he accepted Jesus Christ as his personal Lord and Savior.

The new transmitter had been beaming radio broadcasts around the world for twenty-one months when news arrived that the Japanese had bombed Pearl Harbor in Hawaii on December 7, 1941. In response, the following day the United States declared war on Japan. The United States was now an active participant in the Second World War, which had been going on in Europe and North Africa for two years.

As a result, the programs broadcast by HCJB took on a new urgency, and the staff produced and broadcast the *Service Stripes Hour* to inspire and support the men and women fighting in the armed forces.

The Second World War was also touching Quito. Many German spies had infiltrated the countries of South America, and Ecuador was no exception. Five hundred German soldiers were stationed at the German embassy in Quito, and they liked to march back and forth in a show of force with their swastika armbands clearly visible for all to see. German bombers would circle the city from time to time, dropping leaflets boasting of their intentions to take over the country. It was a tense time, and Clarence and Stuart laid out an evacuation route from the city should the Germans invade. In fact, Clarence was warned one day by a government official.

"We expect a German strike tomorrow," the official said. "Order your men to shoot their families should there be a takeover."

Clarence knew he could never do that, and fortunately the following day the sky above Quito was abuzz with American P47 airplanes, and no German attack occurred.

Clarence was also facing challenges at home. His sixteen-year-old daughter, Marian, was very ill. She had fainted and fallen, banging her head on the concrete curbing in the process and fracturing her skull. A huge blood clot had developed at the site of the injury, and the doctor was unsure whether Marian would ever fully recover from the accident.

He ordered long-term bed rest for her. However, this turned out to be not such an easy thing to enforce on the usually active Marian. It was also difficult for Katherine to take care of her daughter, since she was once again pregnant and in need of a lot of bed rest herself. Clarence did what he could to help his family, making meals between programs and taking one or two of the children at a time to the studio to relieve Katherine of some of her workload.

With all the added stress, Katherine gave birth to the baby early. Clarence took the children up to see their new sister, whom they had named Elizabeth. But all was not well with the child, who died at three days of age. Once again, just as he had thirteen years earlier, Clarence had to arrange a funeral for one of his children. The death of Elizabeth broke his heart, but it did not break his will to keep broadcasting the gospel. With the war raging in Europe and in Asia and the Pacific, Clarence knew that the programs the radio station was broadcasting were the only voice of hope and freedom that many people in those regions could hear.

The work of broadcasting continued at a fast pace, and in 1943 Clarence Moore was invited to attend an international conference of radio technicians being held in New York City. When he returned to Quito, he reported to Clarence that many people at the conference had complimented him and HCJB for being smart enough to locate their radio station on the equator at such a high altitude.

"What do you mean?" Clarence asked.

"Well," Clarence Moore began, "it turns out that the equator is the absolute best location for broadcasting to the northern and southern hemispheres, since the equator is an equal distance from the magnetic poles. It's the location in the world the freest from atmospheric disturbance. And our hundred-foot antenna erected ninety-three hundred feet above sea level is virtually equivalent to having a ten-thousand-foot antenna. The higher above sea level you can get your antenna, the farther your signal will carry around the globe. That's why so many people in so many different countries can pick up our signal."

Clarence Jones chuckled to himself. "No one called us smart when we settled on Quito," he told Clarence Moore. "In fact, the State Department warned us that this was a terrible spot to transmit from. I guess it's better to follow God's leading than man's suggestions, don't you agree?"

Clarence Moore nodded enthusiastically.

Christmas Day 1943 marked Radio HCJB's twelfth year of broadcasting. To mark the occasion, a special twelfth anniversary broadcast went on the air at 4:00 PM on December 25, 1943. Most of those who had been present for the original broadcast twelve years before were present on this day. As Clarence sat shoulder to shoulder with these people, he couldn't help but reminisce. It amazed him to think of the growth of the radio ministry over the past twelve years.

The broadcast was originating from HCJB's beautiful, new, state-of-the-art studio. What a difference it was from the converted living room at

Quinta Corston, where the first broadcast originated. Now there was not only a new studio but also a large office building with plenty of office space for everyone. There was also new housing for the ever-growing staff, which now numbered about twenty-five foreigners and another sixty Ecuadorian men and women who worked either full- or part-time for the station. And the little 200-watt original transmitter had been replaced by a much more powerful one. Back then they had broadcast to the few people with radio receivers in Quito. Today they were broadcasting the anniversary program around the world in a number of different languages.

Soon after celebrating the twelfth anniversary of broadcasting, Clarence received a letter from one of the board members of the World Radio Missionary Fellowship in the United States, encouraging him and the other staff in Quito not to grow complacent with their accomplishments so far. The letter challenged them to keep moving forward, improving what they had already established, and searching and planning for more effective ways to use Christian radio. In part the letter read,

> Here are two facts which stand out in my thinking about planning and building for a better HCJB in the future: 1. HCJB must go forward. I'm sure we're agreed that we dare not rest upon our past blessings or consider ourselves as having "arrived" in any sense. Paul said it right in Philippians 3:13: "Forgetting those things which are behind." 2. HCJB

> will go forward only if we pray and plan for progress. We must not fail in our advantage and special opportunities which seemingly no other group of Christians on earth has at the present time. We must keep "reaching forth unto those things which are before... pressing toward the mark."

Clarence took the letter to heart and began discussing and praying with members of the staff about the next steps the radio ministry should take. Among the goals they felt God was leading them to focus on was a 50,000-watt shortwave transmitter that would improve the reach of their broadcasts even farther around the world.

As he reflected on what had already been done and what lay ahead to do, Clarence observed, "It's amazing what can be accomplished if you're not concerned about who gets the credit."

Chapter 15

Expanding the Ministry

Clarence and the staff at HCJB continued to work hard throughout the years of the Second World War. Many of the staff had relatives living or fighting in combat zones or who had been captured by the Germans or the Japanese and were being held as prisoners of war. While they kept busy with the work of the radio station, they were concerned about their relatives, and everyone let out a sigh of relief in 1945 when first the Germans and then the Japanese surrendered. The Second World War was over, and the Allies had triumphed. Clarence and Katherine threw a huge party at their home to celebrate the end of the war.

Soon after the war ended, poignant letters arrived at the radio station in Quito, telling of the value of Christian radio broadcasts during the war. One such letter came from a New Zealand serviceman named David. David wrote about how he had been captured by the Japanese and held as a prisoner of war on a remote Pacific island. Knowing that David was an electronics specialist, his Japanese captors had brought him some radio parts and demanded that he build them a shortwave radio receiver. David wrote that he had been able to build the receiver, but he'd also had enough spare parts to secretly build himself a miniature radio receiver. He had hidden the radio during the day, and in the middle of the night he would take it out and scan the dial for a station to listen to. His radio picked up HCJB's signal loud and clear. David was so relieved to hear a friendly, encouraging voice coming over the radio that he cried. During the day he would share all he could remember about the broadcast with his fellow prisoners of war, and he would eagerly tune in for more the next night.

The Japanese overseers of the prison were so happy that they could tune in and listen to news from Japan on the radio David had built for them that they had asked what they could bring him as a way of showing their appreciation. David had asked for a Bible, confessing in his letter that this was something he would never have thought of asking for before listening to HCJB. The guards had brought not one but four Bibles, and during the next three and a half years that David was incarcerated in the prisoner-of-war camp, he held regular Bible studies that sustained him and many other prisoners.

From Norway, a very long way from the islands of the Pacific Ocean, another story unfolded. During the war the Nazis had occupied Norway. As a result, many young men and women went underground to resist the occupation of their country. Ole, the writer of the letter that arrived at HCJB in Quito, was one of these young men. He wrote about how, on one dark night in a remote farming area of Norway, he had heard an aircraft flying low overhead. He ran outside to see whether the plane was about to crash just in time to see it circle and then drop a parcel, using a small, white parachute. When Ole retrieved the parcel, it had a note attached to it that read, "Friend, here is a radio receiver as an encouragement from Britain's Royal Air Force." Since the Nazis had banned the private ownership of all radios, receiving a radio this way was a huge surprise to Ole. But the radio was also a dangerous possession. The penalty for being caught with one was death.

Ignoring the danger, Ole had turned on the radio receiver and had been able to tune in to a program broadcast in English by HCJB. He was ecstatic to learn what was happening in other parts of the world. When the broadcast was over, he hid the radio in the barn. Each night he went out to tend to the cows—and tune in the radio. One night as he tuned in the radio, to his delight he picked up a Swedish woman broadcasting from Quito. Ole understood Swedish better than English, and he listened intently to the broadcast. The woman, Ellen Campaña, had said, "We want you to remember,

Christian brothers and sisters in occupied countries, that God loves us and wants us to be filled with love, even for our enemies and those who are oppressing us."

Ole wrote that although he was already a Christian, that broadcast had encouraged him so much that he arranged for a dozen of his friends to meet nightly in the barn to listen to the program with him. The group kept on tuning in right up until the night that Ellen Campaña announced that the Germans had surrendered. The war was over!

Clarence was touched by such stories and gave thanks to God that the broadcasts of Radio HCJB had been able to bless and encourage people during the long, dark days of the Second World War. But he was not ready to rest on his laurels. In typical fashion he saw the end of the war as an opportunity to extend the reach and type of services that HCJB offered. To that end he and the board of directors of the radio station decided that they needed a permanent office in New York City that could serve as a base for promoting their work and for recruiting staff in the United States and Canada. While the office was being established, Clarence and Reuben agreed to rotate between living in Quito and living in New York. This move was made possible because an able young couple, Abe and Delores Van Der Puy, had arrived to take up leadership positions within the team in Quito.

Reuben and his family took the first term in New York. They set up home in a Manhattan apartment and began a rigorous recruiting and publicity campaign. Reuben visited so many churches and summer Bible conferences in the United States and Canada that he lost count of them. Always his message was the same: "Get involved with world evangelism any way you can! Pray, give, or go."

In the two years that Reuben was in the United States, Clarence pushed forward with new plans for the radio station. The biggest issue he had to deal with was finding a plot of land outside Quito on which to situate the new 50,000-watt transmitter. This transmitter would be much too powerful for a permit to be issued for its erection on their present site. In addition, the city was growing rapidly, and it was doubtful whether the Quito Light and Power Company could provide the electricity needed to run it. The plan was to find a parcel of about fifty acres of flat land on which to put the new transmitter and antenna. Preferably the site should be located in the middle of a wide valley so that the surrounding mountains did not interfere with the new antenna's signal. Also, it had to have an adequate water supply. The new transmitter and antenna were going to be powered by diesel generators, and water would be needed to cool them.

Since Quito was located in the Andes, Clarence knew that finding the right piece of land was going to be an interesting challenge. After praying that God would lead them to the right spot, they began their search for the site. It took many months to find it, but finally Clarence heard about a parcel of land for sale at Pifo, about eighteen miles east of Quito. The land was part of a huge farm that had been subdivided into several small farming lots and sold. But because this particular piece of land was not suitable for farming, it had remained unsold. And because it was "useless," it did not cost nearly as much as other similarly sized plots.

Clarence and several members of the engineering staff from the radio station drove out to inspect the property. The site was perfect. It was flat, was located in the center of a broad valley, and had an ample water supply to meet their needs. Three days later Clarence signed the papers to buy the land, which was registered in the name of the World Radio Missionary Fellowship, Inc.

With the land purchased, Clarence's attention turned to raising the money needed to design, build, and install the new 50,000-watt transmitter and antenna. Such an undertaking was not going to be cheap, and money for the project was still being raised in 1948 when the Jones family moved to New York City to man the new HCJB office. Marian, however, chose to stay behind in Quito. She was now twenty-two years old and had a good job, which she did not want to leave, as a secretary at the U.S. embassy.

Once the rest of the family arrived in New York, Clarence did not take the time to settle in. He left that job to Katherine. Instead he set out straightaway on a promotional and recruiting tour of the United States and Canada. While speaking at Peoples

Church in Toronto, Canada, Clarence met a young medical student named Paul Roberts. Paul would soon be graduating from medical school, and he asked Clarence, "Is there any chance that I could join HCJB after I graduate?"

Clarence was thrilled by the question. For some time he had been concerned about the medical needs of the growing staff in Quito. As well, over the years he had watched the Indians traveling the Pan American Highway in and out of Quito. He had noted that these Indians were not always in good health and they had nowhere to go in the area to get medical treatment. When Paul asked whether there was a place for him in HCJB, Clarence quickly sent off a letter to Reuben.

> I've been thinking about the need to have our own medical staff in Quito. A resident doctor could (a) oversee the health of our growing staff, (b) operate a small Indian clinic, (c) carry on an itinerant work with the sound bus, (d) give medical advice on the radio. We might also install a small hospital for missionaries and the public.
>
> If you like the idea, Reu, I think we have just the man, who would be supported by Peoples Church.

Reuben liked the idea, and soon a small house located along the Pan American Highway close by the radio station was rented to be used as a medical clinic, and after his graduation from medical school, Paul moved with his wife to Quito.

In April 1949 Clarence was on hand to witness the opening of the clinic. It was not a splashy start. The ceremony was a small affair, as was the new medical ministry. But as Clarence reminded those who gathered for the opening, HCJB had also started as a tiny operation. Soon, as Clarence had envisaged, Dr. Roberts was busy at the new clinic, taking care of the medical needs of the HCJB staff and the poor Indians who traversed the Pan American Highway.

A month later, in May 1949, Clarence learned that he had been honored in a special way. John Brown University in Siloam Springs, Arkansas, had awarded him an honorary doctorate of laws degree. Clarence was both flattered and a little embarrassed. He realized that being able to use the title Dr. Jones would help open doors for him, but he was concerned that people might think he was a medical doctor, especially with the opening of the clinic in Quito.

Three months later, on August 5, 1949, the medical staff at the new HCJB clinic was put to the test. They were needed—and in a hurry—in Ambato, seventy-five miles to the south. A massive earthquake had struck the town, killing and injuring thousands and almost completely leveling the town. The president of Ecuador phoned and asked Clarence for help. The medical staff were quickly loaded into one of the sound buses and were on their way to the scene of the devastation. Once they arrived in Ambato, the medical team got right to work tending the needs of the many injured people.

HCJB was pressed into service in other ways as well. At 6:30 AM the following day, Ecuador's President Galo Plaza addressed the nation over the radio from the sound bus, informing the citizens of the country about the size and nature of the devastation in Ambato. At least six thousand people were dead, many thousands were injured, and over one hundred thousand people had been left homeless.

Later that day Clarence received a telegram from NBC in New York City, asking if they could arrange a direct radio feed from devastated Ambato. The next day, Sunday, an exhausted President Plaza was broadcasting once again from the sound bus. This time, since the broadcast was connected through HCJB to the NBC, CBS, and Mutual radio networks in the United States, the president was explaining to the world the extent of the devastation in Ambato. The radio hookup brought HCJB to the attention of a whole new segment of the radio-listening public.

The day of this broadcast brought another tragedy to the already devastated region. A Bristol aircraft belonging to the Shell Oil Company was carrying thirty-seven of the company's employees from Shell Mera to Ambato to search for missing relatives, when it crashed into the side of Mount Bolivar, killing everyone aboard.

The plane crash was the last straw for the Shell Oil Company. Shell had spent millions of dollars drilling exploratory wells around the Oriente, but despite its best efforts, it had not found oil in commercial quantities. The difficult living conditions in the jungle and constant harassment from a tribe of savage Indians know as the Aucas had taken a heavy toll on the workers. Many Shell Oil workers had died or been killed in the company's eleven-year search for oil in Ecuador. Now, with the plane crash near Ambato, the company decided to give up its search for oil in the Oriente and pull its operations out of Ecuador.

For Clarence the Ambato earthquake underscored the need to press forward with HCJB's medical work. He was therefore delighted when Dr. Everett Fuller and his wife, Liz, joined the HCJB medical team in Quito.

Not long after the Fullers' arrival in Ecuador, a young missionary named Nate Saint came to Quito on business. Nate and his wife were living at the now-abandoned Shell Oil Company airfield and base of operation at Shell Mera. While in Quito, Nate met with Dr. Fuller and Clarence and posed a question to them. Would Dr. Fuller be prepared to come to Shell Mera and open a clinic that over time could develop into a full-fledged hospital?

Dr. Fuller and his wife jumped at the opportunity to pioneer a medical work in the Oriente. Clarence also embraced the opportunity. He was excited that his and Nate's visions for medical missions in the jungle fit so well together, and the two men agreed that the new clinic should be operated under the ministry umbrella of HCJB.

Just as Clarence had predicted, the post–World War II years turned out to be a boom time for the mission. By 1951 the World Radio Missionary Fellowship had fifty foreign missionaries serving in Quito and at the clinic at Shell Mera, and over one hundred Ecuadorians worked for the organization. But no matter how big the staff, there was always plenty to do.

One of the projects that Clarence turned his attention to was development of the new land they had purchased at Pifo. First the land had to be cleared, and here Clarence led the way. At 6:00 each morning he climbed onto a bulldozer and worked to clear the old cornfield so that construction could begin on a new transmitter building, generating plant, and other utility buildings.

By January 1953 Clarence and Katherine were back in the United States promoting the radio ministry. Their children were nearly all grown. Marian was married to Bob Clark, who was leading the development of the site at Pifo. Marjorie was still in Ecuador, Richard was a decorated Korean War hero, and Nancy was a freshman at Wheaton College in Illinois.

With their family raised, Clarence and Katherine gave 100 percent of their time to the World Radio Missionary Fellowship. Many people asked about working with HCJB, and Clarence always offered the same challenge, "First you need to be totally committed to God, then to the country you are serving in, and finally to the mission. Then you have to be a specialist in one or two areas and be very good at serving others. Bring along a tuxedo or evening gown so that you will be fit to meet the president, and overalls so that you will be fit to do the work."

By January 12 Clarence and Katherine had finished a whirlwind round of speaking engagements on the West Coast and were driving east. They were on the outskirts of Santa Barbara, California, when Clarence decided to pull over for gas. He was just slowing down when a car coming from the opposite direction pulled out to pass a slower vehicle and sped toward Clarence and Katherine's car in their lane. Clarence watched helplessly as the other driver realized his mistake and pulled frantically on his steering wheel. But it was too late. *Bam!* The two cars hit head-on.

Chapter 16

Recovery and Change

Clarence took a deep breath. *The pain has not set in yet,* he told himself. *Do what you can.* Very slowly he turned his head, reached around, and turned off the engine. Then he looked over at Katherine. Her head was embedded in the windshield, and blood was spurting from her forehead.

Clarence heard shouting in the distance, and someone shined a flashlight into the wrecked car. Clarence reached into his pocket and pulled out a notepad and pencil. Then, although he could not properly see what he was writing, he scribbled down "Romans 8:28," tore the page from the notebook, and grasped it in his hand. *There,* he thought. *When I die, they will know what my last thoughts were. Maybe they will even preach them at my funeral.* Romans 8:28 read,

"And we know that all things work together for good to them that love God, to them who are called according to his purpose."

"She's dead." Clarence heard the words and was vaguely aware that the person who said them was talking about Katherine.

"The two in the other car are gone, too. Looks like this man is the only survivor. Let's get him out of here, boys," someone else said.

Clarence heard the door being wrenched open and felt strong arms pulling him free of the wreckage and onto a waiting gurney. After that it was hard for him to concentrate. Painkillers were shot into his arm, and when he arrived at Santa Barbara Hospital, he was whisked straight into surgery. When he awoke, his entire face was a ball of bandages. He had no way to open his mouth to speak. Clarence soon found out why. His jaw had been shattered by the impact on the steering wheel and windshield. The surgeon had counted forty-two separate pieces of shattered jawbone and had threaded them together on a wire while they healed and the bone knit back together.

Clarence motioned for a piece of paper. "Where is Katherine?" he wrote.

The nurse smiled weakly. "Can you hear me?" she asked.

Clarence lifted his hand to indicate that he could hear.

"Okay then, Mr. Jones. I need to tell you that your wife is alive, but she is very seriously injured.

I will ask the doctor if I can wheel your bed into her room so that you can see her."

Soon Clarence was being wheeled down the hospital corridor. Although no one said it out loud, he had the distinct feeling that the staff were not expecting Katherine to live much longer and they were setting up one last encounter between him and his wife of twenty-nine years.

Clarence would never have recognized Katherine. She was hooked up to various tubes and monitors as she lay unconscious. Clarence lay in his bed beside her, praying and waiting for her to wake up. She did not.

One day passed, and then two, and three. "Frankly," the doctor finally told Clarence, "it might be better if she stays in the coma and slips away from there. The EEG shows so much brain damage that she would have massive problems if she regained consciousness. She will never be able to feed herself or think clearly again. And it looks like we are going to have to amputate her feet. They are too mangled to ever be restored by surgery."

Clarence heard what the doctor was saying, but he refused to believe it. By now Richard was at his bedside, and silently father and son prayed for Katherine's recovery. Richard also sent out messages asking for additional prayer, and soon HCJB was beaming the prayer request around the world. With so much prayer being offered up for his wife, Clarence was sure that her condition would improve.

On the ninth day Katherine did open her eyes and mumble. Clarence was right by her side and squeezed her hand tightly.

Katherine looked at him intently. "Why, you're not the Lord!" she exclaimed and slipped back into her coma.

From then on Katherine slipped in and out of consciousness. Two weeks later Clarence made the decision to have her and himself transferred to the Presbyterian Medical Center in New York City. He had learned that this was the best place for him to have more surgery on his shattered jaw.

The doctor had decided to postpone amputating Katherine's feet, and her legs and feet were encased in heavy plaster casts. Her head was bandaged, as was Clarence's, and Clarence knew they made quite a sight as they were loaded onto the airplane for the flight to New York. Richard accompanied them on the flight, and Nancy was waiting to meet them in New York.

When they finally arrived at Presbyterian Medical Center, a specialist took a look at Clarence's jaw and declared, "I don't think you will ever be able to talk again."

"How about play the trombone?" Clarence wrote in response.

The specialist shook his head. "No way that's going to happen either," he said.

Clarence refused to believe what the doctor said, even after a second operation on his jaw and despite the fact that he had to suck baby food through a straw for sustenance.

Slowly and painfully both Clarence and Katherine began to heal. Forty-two days passed before they were released from the hospital with strict instructions for complete bed rest at home.

Katherine's sister Ruth and her brother-in-law Chet picked them up from the hospital and took them to Talcottville, Connecticut, where HCJB had just bought a guest house. Katherine still had casts on both legs and was so heavily drugged that it was hard to tell how much her brain was functioning. Clarence was still in much pain, too, but now that the wire had been taken out of his jaw, he was determined to get his facial movements back.

Clarence put his total focus on his and Katherine's recovery, and step-by-step, progress was made. Katherine had the casts removed from her legs and feet and was slowly able to relearn the skill of walking. Meanwhile Clarence practiced moving his jaw and mouth each day until he could unclench his teeth enough to mumble, then talk, then whistle, and finally play the trombone.

Katherine's recovery, though, was much less predictable. The strong drugs took away her will to live, and days went by with her sitting on the sofa, staring listlessly out the window. Clarence talked to her about what was happening back in Quito and encouraged her to imagine a bright future for them as a couple. Thankfully the brain damage did not leave as much permanent disability as the doctor expected, and Katherine had recovered enough to be mother of the bride when Marjorie married Marvin Steffins six months later.

By the time Clarence and Katherine were well enough to travel back to Ecuador, it was October 1955. On their way to Ecuador they stopped off in Panama to visit Clarence's brother Howard and his wife, Lillian, who were now helping to run radio station HOXO, a local Christian radio station that had been taken over by HCJB.

The Joneses arrived back in Quito just in time for the opening of the Rimmer Memorial Hospital in the city. This was HCJB's latest venture built under the direction of Dr. Paul Roberts. Clarence was impressed with what he saw. The hospital was a two-storied structure, with offices and an outpatient department on the bottom floor. The second floor housed the operating room, maternity rooms, and other wards. Paul explained that the hospital could accommodate thirty patients at a time and fifteen newborn babies.

The staff at the radio station had also grown considerably in the time Clarence and Katherine were away, leaving many new missionaries and national workers for the couple to get acquainted with.

Not long after Clarence returned to Quito, Nate Saint, Missionary Aviation Fellowship's pilot in the Oriente, flew into the city. As usual he visited Clarence, and the two men began talking about life in the jungle. Nate explained how the HCJB clinic at

Shell Mera was a real blessing, not only to the missionaries in the area but also to the local Indian population. He looked forward to the clinic's growing into a full-fledged hospital and told Clarence that he and another young missionary serving in the area, Jim Elliot, had begun work on the building to house the new hospital.

A month later, on January 8, 1956, five young missionaries, including Nate Saint and Jim Elliot, were reported missing in the Ecuadorian jungle. It was gravely feared that the five of them had been killed by the Aucas, the same savage Stone Age tribe that had in the past harassed and killed a number of workers for the Shell Oil Company.

When Clarence heard that Nate and four other missionaries were missing, he dispatched Abe Van Der Puy to Shell Mera to help with the search-and-recovery operation. Clarence remained in Quito to relay reports from Abe to the radio station's worldwide audience. Three days later Abe reported that it had been confirmed that the five missing missionaries were all dead. The Aucas had speared them to death on the banks of the Curaray River. Suddenly HCJB was besieged with reporters from around the world, wanting to know what had become of the missionaries, why they had gone on such a dangerous mission, and whether any others planned to follow them. Clarence took the opportunity to share the hope of eternity with them all.

As a result of the death of the five missionaries, many people became interested in seeing Nate Saint's vision for an HCJB hospital at Shell Mera come to fruition. Money began to flow in from around the world for the project, and *Back to the Bible* radio commentator Theodore Epp also took up the challenge of raising money for the venture.

Despite the sad beginning to 1956, Christmas that year was a great encouragement to Clarence and the workers at HCJB. Christmas Day 1956 marked the twenty-fifth anniversary of HCJB. Ecuadorian President Galo Plaza presided over the anniversary celebration and ended the event by encouraging the staff with the words, "I hope you are here to remain with us forever. I am sure that is the heartfelt wish of all Ecuadorians."

During the anniversary celebration, Dr. Carlos Andrade Marin, the mayor of Quito, also gave a speech. Afterward he and Clarence reminisced about how, as a young secretary for the president of Ecuador, Carlos had kept placing HCJB's application for a radio license on the top of the pile of papers on the president's desk.

The twenty-fifth anniversary also marked the inauguration of the new 50,000-watt transmitter and antenna at Pifo, once again extending the reach of HCJB's signal around the world.

The next milestone occurred in May 1958, when Clarence and many others gathered to dedicate the new twenty-bed Epp Memorial Hospital at Shell Mera. Theodore Epp, who had helped raise so much money for the project, was on hand to unveil a commemorative plaque that read,

Voice of the Andes Hospital
of the eastern jungle in Shell
Dedicated to the Glory of God
May 10, 1958
"NOT BY MIGHT NOR BY POWER,
BUT BY MY SPIRIT"

By now Clarence was fifty-seven years old, and the car accident had made him think about handing over the leadership responsibilities of HCJB to someone younger. As he looked around for the right person, he noted, "I'm looking for aptitude, attitude, and action; for a person who has spiritual impulse, the certainty of God's motivation that will carry him on in spite of the obstacles. I'm looking for someone who is willing to work harder than anyone else and who won't ask anyone else to do what he is not willing to do himself. Leadership is the ability to follow up on what you think should be done. It takes guts, tenacity, and stick-to-it-iveness."

It was clear to Clarence as he looked around that Abe Van Der Puy fit the criteria. Clarence approached the board of directors and discussed with them the idea of grooming Abe as his replacement. The board agreed, and Clarence began the process of handing over his day-to-day leadership role to a younger man.

The growing ministry continued to face new challenges. Television was the latest technical innovation, and Marian and her husband, Bob Clark, were put to work pioneering Christian TV programs that HCJB could broadcast. In addition, the roster of languages the radio station broadcast in continued to grow.

Before Clarence stepped down from his position, the board of directors had one last request of him. They wanted Clarence to go on a world tour of missionary radio stations to stir up interest in Christian radio and report back on how they could all work together more closely.

Clarence was delighted with this assignment, especially since Katherine now felt well enough to join him on the thirteen-month trip. The couple set out from Quito in late 1958 to travel through South America. Everywhere Clarence went, he spoke and conducted seminars on "How to produce radio programs" and "Radio, the new missionary."

From South America Clarence and Katherine headed north through the Caribbean islands and up the East Coast of the United States. While in the United States, Clarence was particularly gratified to find that Lance Latham had taken the boys' and girls' clubs they had started together at the Chicago Gospel Tabernacle years before and turned them into a national network of Christian children's clubs. Lance had called the clubs Awanas and credited Clarence as the founder of them. "Nothing you do for God is wasted," Clarence told Katherine as they visited one of the clubs to tell the children about their work in Quito.

From the United States Clarence and Katherine sailed for Europe, then traveled on to Africa, Israel,

India, Thailand, Cambodia, and Singapore. Everywhere Clarence went, he tried to show the value of radio in reaching with the gospel into difficult areas where there were people who would not go inside a Christian church. He also took a shortwave receiver along with him on the trip, and each night he and Katherine would tune in to see what was happening back in Quito. Even in places as remote as Irian Jaya and the hills of Western Australia, the signal was strong enough for clear reception. Often Clarence and Katherine would hold hands and marvel at the amazing things they had accomplished in their twenty-seven years with Radio HCJB.

In November 1961 Clarence and Katherine returned to Quito, where it was time for Clarence to hand over the role of president of the organization to Abe Van Der Puy. Abe had already proved himself by doing a great job of running the operation while Clarence was traveling, and so it was not difficult for Clarence to hand the reins of leadership over to Abe.

The board of directors did not want Clarence to retire altogether, however, and neither did Clarence. Instead they appointed him Ambassador at Large for the World Christian Radio Fellowship and asked him and Katherine to do as much speaking around the world as they could. The arrangement suited Clarence well, and he had soon set up a rigorous schedule for speaking engagements at Bible conferences and church meetings.

The years rolled by, and the Jones family spread out across the American continent. Marian and Bob Clark stayed on in Quito with their three children. Richard and his wife, Carol, moved with their four children to Panama, where Richard helped run radio station HOXO. Nancy married a man from Chicago named Bob Sutherlin, and they produced three children in quick succession, while Marjorie and Marvin Steffins had six children. A total of sixteen grandchildren kept Granny and Grandpa Jones very busy!

The entire family were able to get together in June 1965, and Clarence was proud of them all. But one year and one month later, tragedy struck the family. Richard crashed his van while driving in a blinding rainstorm in Panama. He was thrown from the vehicle in the accident and died a day later. Clarence and Katherine rushed to Panama to be with him in his last hours and to help with the funeral. It was a sad moment for both of them. Now three of their children were dead, and three were alive. Still, Clarence did not let the grief overtake him. He had more work to do, and he vowed to plug away as long as he had the strength to do so.

Chapter 17

Continuing on the Uphill Journey

Clarence had been on hand in April 1965 when HCJB completed a huge hydroelectric power plant. The plant was situated at Papallacta, where it took water from the headwaters of the Amazon River and produced 1.8 million watts of power for the radio station. Abe Van Der Puy had told Clarence that the cost of the power plant would be covered in five years by the money saved in diesel fuel to run the generators at Pifo. Soon, however, the engineers at the radio station realized that during drought times not enough water was flowing in the river to enter the penstock and turn the turbine to produce power.

Clarence carefully studied the options to correct the problem and agreed with the board of directors when they recommended that a hydro dam be built to create a reservoir from which the water to drive the turbines could be drawn. This was a mammoth task, involving 250 workers and 110 tons of supplies, mostly bags of cement, which had to be loaded onto mules and carried over a dangerous six-mile trail to the dam site. The building of the dam was finally completed in March 1971, and in the time the dam was being built, over half of the workers involved in the project became Christians. Clarence stood proudly with these workers as the new dam was dedicated.

At that time other changes were taking place. Radio was evolving, and more and more people were tuning in to the latest technology—FM stereo radio. HCJB applied to the government for FM frequencies in Quito and Guayaquil, and these were granted. As a result, HCJB-2 was born. This was an easy-listening station that mixed short gospel segments with classical music and popular songs. The station was an instant hit, and Abe sent Clarence an early review of the station by a newspaper reporter in Guayaquil. The review read in part,

> Suddenly, by chance, we found enchanting music and cultured, pleasant voices of a calm and measured kind, with pleasant modulation and proven experience. I am speaking of the new radio station HCJB-2, which begins its broadcast at 12:00 noon and signs off, unfortunately, at 10:00 PM....

> These broadcasts are never interrupted by any kind of commercial advertising. Only once every half-hour there is a short, pithy, as well as agreeable, commentary on peace, human dignity and the virtues which men are forgetting. These never in any way are in the form of a dull sermon. Sometimes they are short, pleasing stories in the form of parables. And thus they introduce Christ to your spirit and "oblige" you to meditate.
>
> They do not proselytize. They mention no specific religion. They only quote short, instructive passages from the Bible in a brief interval between each half-hour of moving, beautiful music. HCJB-2 FM stereo is a great factor in lifting the cultural level of our citizens in general. It has come to fill a real need.

As Clarence read the review, he was very pleased. His mind went back to 1930, when he, Reuben Larson, and John Clark had set out the guidelines for the proposed radio station. The men had declared that the station would always present a positive, hopeful gospel message and that it would stay away from political and denominational issues. It was gratifying to Clarence to know that a new generation of missionary broadcasters had embraced and continued to follow these founding principles.

Radio HCJB continued to face new challenges. One that particularly troubled Clarence was the continual jamming of foreign radio transmissions by the

Communist government of the Soviet Union, with its own huge 500,000-watt shortwave transmitter. At a time when the people of the Soviet Union most needed the gospel beamed to them, the message was being stopped.

Clarence thought and prayed about what to do about the situation, and when he felt he had an answer, he spoke up at the World Christian Radio Fellowship board meeting. "Men, are we going to let the Communists drown out the gospel of Jesus Christ?" he chided. "We'll never win the war with one gun. If they have a 500,000-watt transmitter, what's to stop us from having one as well? We'll send over a barrage they can't ignore."

No one spoke.

"I'll head up the fundraising!" Clarence offered. "If God is in this idea, we will prevail."

And prevail they did. Even though Clarence was seventy-three years old, he attacked the project with as much enthusiasm and vigor as a thirty-three-year-old. He aimed his appeal for the $750,000 needed for the transmitter at supporters in Great Britain. The people rose to the occasion, and the money poured in. In 1975 a team of twelve HCJB engineers was assigned to design, build, and install a 500,000-watt shortwave transmitter. It was an enormous task, and Clarence visited and encouraged the engineers whenever he could.

That same year Clarence went to Washington, D.C., to accept a very special award. The National

Religious Broadcasters organization made Clarence Jones the first inductee into the Religious Broadcasting Hall of Fame and gave him the title of Pioneer Missionary Radio Statesman. Also in that same year, the Clarence Jones Lectureship in Christian Communications was established at Wheaton College in Illinois. The awards and accolades provided a time for Clarence to look back with satisfaction and humility: satisfaction at what had been achieved and humility that God had chosen him to lead such a talented team of workers for so many years.

After Clarence was inducted into the Religious Broadcasting Hall of Fame, many people expected him to retire from active Christian service, especially since he and Katherine had bought a small house in Largo, Florida. But Clarence had other plans.

Four weeks after his induction into the hall of fame, Clarence was in Canada, meeting with the leaders of five other missions: Overseas Missionary Fellowship, Latin American Mission, Africa Inland Mission, the Oriental Missionary Society, and the Sudan Interior Mission. Clarence saw a great opportunity and suggested that the leaders of the six organizations travel together through Canada, promoting missions and jointly presenting the needs of each of their organizations.

The tour was very successful and was immensely rewarding for Clarence. The idea of different men and women from various mission organizations standing together to promote the needs of their organizations in presenting the gospel reflected his highest hopes for Christian work.

After the tour of Canada, Clarence and Katherine traveled to Nome, Alaska, where they met with Peter Deyneka of the Slavic Gospel Mission. For many years Peter had been broadcasting gospel shows in Russian over HCJB, and now he and Clarence were guest speakers at a mission conference in Nome.

Clarence listened with rapt interest as Peter spoke of some of the Christians he had encountered on his covert trips into the Soviet Union. Peter told of meeting three Soviet army officers who were posted to a base in Siberia. The officers played with their shortwave radio set on the long, frozen nights and eventually came across HCJB's Russian program. At first they listened skeptically, but soon they were singing and praying along. Three months later they sought out an underground church many miles away and walked to it. When they arrived at the church, they told the congregation, "We have come to know the Lord through the shortwave radio, and now we wish to fellowship with you."

Peter reported that many Soviet Christians had told him, "We feel God invented radio just for us!"

When Clarence stood up to speak, he started with that thought. "There is a genius of broadcasting that fits Scripture perfectly. When Psalm 19 talks about the heavens declaring the glory of God, 'Their line is gone out through all the earth, and their words to the end of the world.' This is radio that the psalmist is talking about. I believe radio was in the mind of God from the very beginning."

In 1981 Clarence and Katherine journeyed south to Quito to celebrate the Fiftieth Jubilee of HCJB. It was a glorious moment for them, to be looking back over fifty years of service and catching a glimpse of the bright future. The 500,000-watt transmitter had been installed at Pifo, doubling the station's transmitting power to one million watts! HCJB now had offices in twenty countries, and in Quito alone there were 250 full-time foreign missionaries and 300 nationals working for the ministry. In Heralding Christ Jesus' Blessings throughout the world, HCJB broadcast six programs simultaneously, twenty-four hours a day, in fifteen languages.

Everyone at the jubilee wanted to meet Clarence and shake his hand, and sometimes it was difficult for Clarence to get through the crowd to see what he wanted to see. He was particularly interested in touring the well-stocked HCJB bookstore and the Rimmer Hospital, which had just been expanded yet again. He visited the Quinta Corston, and as he did so, the years rolled away, and it seemed like yesterday that they had inaugurated the first broadcast from there.

On the trip to the Fiftieth Jubilee, Clarence had to admit that his eighty-one-year-old body had slowed down a little, but he vowed to continue doing what he could. "I have always been looking up," he told the assembled crowd. "Even in my darkest days, I have made it my goal, my personal challenge, to climb upward. And I am not through yet. I pray that God will never set me aside on the shelf, that I will never know what it is to be a dry Christian, like a river with nothing but rocks. Old age is about challenges and climbing upward, not going downhill but uphill."

For the next five years Clarence continued his journey uphill, preaching where he could, writing countless letters to encourage missionaries and friends, praying often for his daughters and sixteen grandchildren, and conducting a local Bible study. But all journeys must end, and Clarence Jones's extraordinary journey ended on April 29, 1986, when he died quietly in his sleep at home in Largo, Florida.

Fittingly, news of Clarence's passing was beamed around the world on the radio waves of HCJB. Soon messages of Christian love and sympathy were pouring in to Katherine from such faraway places as the Soviet Union, the Philippines, and Egypt.

In 1927 Clarence Jones had felt God challenge him to set out to reach the ends of the world with Christian radio. Fifty-nine years later, the messages of condolence that flowed in upon news of his death were proof enough that he had stuck unswervingly to that task.

Bibliography

Boyes, Eleanor. *Bridge to the Rain Forest.* HCJB World Radio, 1995.

Catch the Vision: The Story of HCJB, the Voice of the Andes. World Radio Missionary Fellowship, Inc., 1989.

Cook, Frank S. *Seeds in the Wind.* World Radio Missionary Fellowship, Inc., 1981.

Jones, Clarence W. *Radio, the New Missionary.* Chicago: Moody Press, 1946.

Neely, Lois. *Come Up to This Mountain: The Miracle of Clarence W. Jones & HCJB.* Wheaton, Ill.: Tyndale House Publishers, 1980.

About the Authors

Janet and Geoff Benge are a husband and wife writing team with more than thirty years of writing experience. Janet is a former elementary school teacher. Geoff holds a degree in history. Originally from New Zealand, the Benges spent ten years serving with Youth With A Mission. They have two daughters, Laura and Shannon, and an adopted son, Lito. They make their home in the Orlando, Florida, area.

Also from Janet and Geoff Benge...

More adventure-filled biographies for ages 10 to 100!

Christian Heroes: Then and Now

Gladys Aylward: The Adventure of a Lifetime • 978-1-57658-019-6
Nate Saint: On a Wing and a Prayer • 978-1-57658-017-2
Hudson Taylor: Deep in the Heart of China • 978-1-57658-016-5
Amy Carmichael: Rescuer of Precious Gems • 978-1-57658-018-9
Eric Liddell: Something Greater Than Gold • 978-1-57658-137-7
Corrie ten Boom: Keeper of the Angels' Den • 978-1-57658-136-0
William Carey: Obliged to Go • 978-1-57658-147-6
George Müller: Guardian of Bristol's Orphans • 978-1-57658-145-2
Jim Elliot: One Great Purpose • 978-1-57658-146-9
Mary Slessor: Forward into Calabar • 978-1-57658-148-3
David Livingstone: Africa's Trailblazer • 978-1-57658-153-7
Betty Greene: Wings to Serve • 978-1-57658-152-0
Adoniram Judson: Bound for Burma • 978-1-57658-161-2
Cameron Townsend: Good News in Every Language • 978-1-57658-164-3
Jonathan Goforth: An Open Door in China • 978-1-57658-174-2
Lottie Moon: Giving Her All for China • 978-1-57658-188-9
John Williams: Messenger of Peace • 978-1-57658-256-5
William Booth: Soup, Soap, and Salvation • 978-1-57658-258-9
Rowland Bingham: Into Africa's Interior • 978-1-57658-282-4
Ida Scudder: Healing Bodies, Touching Hearts • 978-1-57658-285-5
Wilfred Grenfell: Fisher of Men • 978-1-57658-292-3
Lillian Trasher: The Greatest Wonder in Egypt • 978-1-57658-305-0
Loren Cunningham: Into All the World • 978-1-57658-199-5
Florence Young: Mission Accomplished • 978-1-57658-313-5
Sundar Singh: Footprints Over the Mountains • 978-1-57658-318-0
C.T. Studd: No Retreat • 978-1-57658-288-6
Rachel Saint: A Star in the Jungle • 978-1-57658-337-1
Brother Andrew: God's Secret Agent • 978-1-57658-355-5
Clarence Jones: Mr. Radio • 978-1-57658-343-2
Count Zinzendorf: Firstfruit • 978-1-57658-262-6
John Wesley: The World His Parish • 978-1-57658-382-1
C. S. Lewis: Master Storyteller • 978-1-57658-385-2
David Bussau: Facing the World Head-on • 978-1-57658-415-6
Jacob DeShazer: Forgive Your Enemies • 978-1-57658-475-0
Isobel Kuhn: On the Roof of the World • 978-1-57658-497-2
Elisabeth Elliot: Joyful Surrender • 978-1-57658-513-9
D. L. Moody: Bringing Souls to Christ • 978-1-57658-552-8
Paul Brand: Helping Hands • 978-1-57658-536-8
Dietrich Bonhoeffer: In the Midst of Wickedness • 978-1-57658-713-3
Francis Asbury: Circuit Rider • 978-1-57658-737-9

Samuel Zwemer: The Burden of Arabia • 978-1-57658-738-6
Klaus-Dieter John: Hope in the Land of the Incas • 978-1-57658-826-2
Mildred Cable: Through the Jade Gate • 978-1-57658-886-4
John Flynn: Into the Never Never • 978-1-57658-898-7
Richard Wurmbrand: Love Your Enemies • 978-1-57658-987-8
Charles Mulli: We Are Family • 978-1-57658-894-9
John Newton: Change of Heart • 978-1-57658-909-0
Helen Roseveare: Mama Luka • 978-1-57658-910-6
Norman Grubb: Mission Builder • 978-1-57658-915-1
Albert Schweitzer • 978-1-57658-961-8

Heroes of History

George Washington Carver: From Slave to Scientist • 978-1-883002-78-7
Abraham Lincoln: A New Birth of Freedom • 978-1-883002-79-4
Meriwether Lewis: Off the Edge of the Map • 978-1-883002-80-0
George Washington: True Patriot • 978-1-883002-81-7
William Penn: Liberty and Justice for All • 978-1-883002-82-4
Harriet Tubman: Freedombound • 978-1-883002-90-9
John Adams: Independence Forever • 978-1-883002-50-3
Clara Barton: Courage under Fire • 978-1-883002-51-0
Daniel Boone: Frontiersman • 978-1-932096-09-5
Theodore Roosevelt: An American Original • 978-1-932096-10-1
Douglas MacArthur: What Greater Honor • 978-1-932096-15-6
Benjamin Franklin: Live Wire • 978-1-932096-14-9
Christopher Columbus: Across the Ocean Sea • 978-1-932096-23-1
Laura Ingalls Wilder: A Storybook Life • 978-1-932096-32-3
Orville Wright: The Flyer • 978-1-932096-34-7
Captain John Smith: A Foothold in the New World • 978-1-932096-36-1
Thomas Edison: Inspiration and Hard Work • 978-1-932096-37-8
Alan Shepard: Higher and Faster • 978-1-932096-41-5
Ronald Reagan: Destiny at His Side • 978-1-932096-65-1
Davy Crockett: Ever Westward • 978-1-932096-67-5
Milton Hershey: More Than Chocolate • 978-1-932096-82-8
Billy Graham: America's Pastor • 978-1-62486-024-9
Ben Carson: A Chance at Life • 978-1-62486-034-8
Louis Zamperini: Redemption • 978-1-62486-049-2
Elizabeth Fry: Angel of Newgate • 978-1-62486-064-5
William Wilberforce: Take Up the Fight • 978-1-62486-057-7
William Bradford: Plymouth's Rock • 978-1-62486-092-8
Ernest Shackleton: Going South • 978-1-62486-093-5
Benjamin Rush: The Common Good • 978-1-62486-123-9
Dwight Eisenhower: Supreme Commander • 978-1-62486-142-0